Bon Appétit®

Quick & Delicious

THE CONDÉ NAST PUBLICATIONS INC.

Quick & Delicious

Introduction

As readers of Bon Appétit discover in every issue of the magazine, the words "quick" and "delicious" are not mutually exclusive. Some of the most intriguing, satisfying and even spectacular recipes can take mere minutes to prepare.

Which is wonderful news for those of us who lead busy lives and love good food. Whether you're a working single with even less time than money, a two-career couple who love to entertain, a parent endlessly chauffeuring the kids to soccer practice and music lessons and play dates, or an active senior who'd rather linger on the golf course than in the kitchen, having a wealth of quick, delicious recipes close at hand can make a big difference in the quality of your life.

That's why we take great pleasure in presenting to you Quick & Delicious, a collection of recipes specially selected from the pages of Bon Appétit. Some of them come from our popular "Too Busy to Cook?" column, in which readers of the magazine share their favorite timesaving recipes. Others represent a department whose title is eminently self-explanatory: "30-Minute Main Courses." Still more were chosen from the frequent feature stories that aim to help home cooks beat the clock. Whatever their sources, all of the recipes have been tested in Bon Appétit's own kitchen and are guaranteed to give you great results.

To help you plan complete menus or select just the right dish for your needs, the recipes are organized into separate chapters on Appetizers & Beverages, Soups & Salads, Main Courses, Accompaniments and Desserts. You'll also find scattered throughout the book a wealth of cooking tips and hints, as well as suggestions for great ready-to-serve foods we've discovered during the past year. All these grace notes come from the magazine's pages as well, where they appeared in such informative departments as "Starters," "Flavors of the World," "Bon Vivant" and "Ask Bon Appétit."

All these elements have one common goal: to make it as easy as possible for you to put delicious food on your table in as little time as it takes to lift your glass and say, "Bon Appétit."

Bon Appétit®

Quick & Delicious

CONTENTS

Introduction   i

Appetizers & Beverages   1
*Delicious tidbits and drinks to make in moments
and enjoy at leisure.*

Soups & Salads   19
*Fragrant bowlfuls and flavorful salads whose
great taste belies their easy preparation.*

Main Courses   35
*Outstanding centerpieces for the dinner table that
take just minutes to make.*

Accompaniments   73
All the trimmings you need, from vegetables
and potatoes to grains and breads.

Desserts   89
A winning selection of temptations made in
almost less time than it takes to eat them.

Index   96

Acknowledgements & Credits   102

Appetizers & Beverages

The quickest way to make a good impression at any meal is to offer a thoughtfully selected appetizer. Indeed, you could compose an entire meal of such tempting tidbits as Blue Cheese Dip with Pecans, Artichoke Bruschetta, Smoked-Salmon Pizza with Red Onion and Dill or Chicken and Mushroom Quesadillas. To complement them, offer a selection of stylish beverages like Mango-Boysenberry Mimosa, Southwestern Bloody Mary or Blended Citrus Gin Fizz.

Appetizers

CAESAR DIP WITH CRUDITÉS

Over the Fourth of July weekend in 1924, a group of unexpected guests arrived at Caesar's Palace restaurant in Tijuana, Mexico. Running low on food, the owner, Caesar Cardini, threw together a salad with ingredients he had on hand. He made a thick dressing with a coddled egg, garlic-flavored oil, lemon juice, grated cheese and Worcestershire, which added a taste of anchovy. This dip has all the flavors of that first Caesar salad, and romaine lettuce and fresh veggies are nice "dippers."

8 TO 10 APPETIZER SERVINGS

1 cup mayonnaise
½ cup sour cream
½ cup freshly grated Parmesan
 cheese
1 tablespoon fresh lemon juice
1 garlic clove, pressed
1 anchovy fillet, mashed

 Small romaine leaves
 Assorted fresh vegetables

Mix first 6 ingredients in small bowl. Season dip with salt and pepper.
 Serve with lettuce and vegetables.

ASPARAGUS AND SUGAR SNAP PEAS WITH HONEY-MUSTARD DIP

12 SERVINGS

1¼ pounds asparagus, trimmed
1¼ pounds sugar snap peas, trimmed

6 tablespoons Dijon mustard
⅓ cup fresh lemon juice
⅓ cup honey
¼ cup white wine vinegar
¼ cup chopped fresh dill
½ cup olive oil

Bring large pot of water to boil. Add asparagus and blanch 2 minutes. Add sugar snap peas and blanch until vegetables are crisp-tender, about 1 minute longer. Drain. Transfer to large bowl of ice water and cool. Drain vegetables; pat dry.
 Mix mustard, lemon juice, honey, vinegar and dill in medium bowl. Gradually whisk in oil. Season to taste with salt and pepper. (*Vegetables and dipping sauce can be made 1 day ahead. Cover separately and chill. Before serving, bring dip to room temperature and rewhisk to blend.*)
 Place dip in bowl; set on platter. Surround with vegetables.

CRUNCH TIME

Sure, the rosemary-olive oil potato chips from Good Health are sophisticated and delicious; but they also contain 30 percent less fat than regular chips. Call 516-261-2139 for information.

Blue Cheese Dip with Pecans

Many kinds of vegetables and even some fruits go well with this versatile dip.

MAKES ABOUT 3 CUPS

1 8-ounce package cream cheese, room temperature
2 cups purchased refrigerated blue cheese dressing
1⅓ cups chopped pecans, toasted
½ cup crumbled blue cheese (about 4 ounces)

Assorted cut-up fresh vegetables and fruits (such as carrots, bell peppers, celery, broccoli, apples and small clusters of grapes)

Beat cream cheese in medium bowl until smooth. Beat in dressing. Stir in 1 cup pecans and crumbled blue cheese. Season to taste with salt and pepper. Transfer dip to decorative bowl. Sprinkle remaining pecans around edges of dip. (*Can be made 1 day ahead. Cover and chill.*)

Set dip in center of platter. Surround with cut-up vegetables and fruits; serve.

Grilled Bread Topped with Arugula, Goat Cheese, Olives and Onions

12 SERVINGS

9 ounces soft fresh goat cheese (such as Montrachet)
6 teaspoons grated orange peel

9 tablespoons olive oil
6 tablespoons orange juice
2 small red onions (about 1 pound), sliced into ¼-inch-thick rounds

12 4 x 2½ x ⅓-inch diagonal slices sourdough baguette

4 cups fresh arugula leaves, trimmed

¾ cup Kalamata olives or other brine-cured black olives (about 5 ounces), pitted, halved

Mix cheese and 4 teaspoons peel in small bowl. Season with salt and pepper. (*Can be made 1 day ahead. Cover and chill.*)

Prepare barbecue (medium-high heat). Whisk 6 tablespoons oil, orange juice and 2 teaspoons orange peel in 13x9x2-inch glass dish. Season dressing with salt and pepper. Add onions; turn to coat. Using metal spatula, transfer onions to grill and cook until tender and golden, turning occasionally and keeping onions intact, about 10 minutes. Return onions to dressing in dish; turn to coat. Set aside.

Brush remaining 3 tablespoons oil over bread. Grill until bread is golden, about 2 minutes per side. Spread cheese mixture over warm bread.

Add arugula to dressing; toss to coat. Top cheese bread with arugula, onions and olives.

CRUDITÉS WITH ASIAN-STYLE DIP

Look for rice vinegar in the Asian foods section of your market.

MAKES 1 CUP DIP

½ cup mayonnaise
¼ cup sour cream
2 tablespoons soy sauce
2 tablespoons chopped fresh basil
1 tablespoon oriental sesame oil
1 tablespoon toasted sesame seeds
1 tablespoon rice vinegar
1 teaspoon minced peeled fresh ginger
1 teaspoon sugar
½ teaspoon dry mustard
⅛ teaspoon cayenne pepper

Assorted cut-up vegetables (such as carrots, red bell peppers, sugar snap peas, cucumbers and broccoli)

Combine first 11 ingredients in small bowl; whisk to blend. Season dip with salt and pepper. *(Can be prepared 1 day ahead. Cover and refrigerate.)*

Place bowl with dip in center of platter. Surround with assorted vegetables and serve.

CAMEMBERT WITH BLUE CHEESE, FIGS AND PORT SAUCE

4 SERVINGS

1 8-ounce (4½-inch-diameter) firm Camembert cheese with rind
1 large egg, beaten to blend
1 cup fresh breadcrumbs made from crustless French bread
1 cup ruby Port
1 cup dried black Mission figs, halved lengthwise
1 tablespoon sugar

2 tablespoons (¼ stick) butter
⅓ cup crumbled blue cheese
Chopped fresh chives
1 French bread baguette, sliced into rounds, lightly toasted

Brush Camembert on all sides with egg, then coat with breadcrumbs. Place on foil-lined plate and cover.

Bring Port to simmer in heavy small saucepan over medium heat. Add figs; simmer until slightly softened, about 5 minutes. Using slotted spoon, transfer figs to small bowl. Add sugar to Port in pan; boil until reduced to thick syrup, stirring occasionally, about 5 minutes. Pour syrup over figs. *(Cheese and figs can be prepared 3 hours ahead. Refrigerate cheese. Let figs stand at room temperature.)*

Melt butter in heavy skillet over medium-high heat. Add Camembert and cook until breadcrumbs are brown and cheese is warm, about 2 minutes per side. Transfer to platter. Top with blue cheese, figs and syrup. Sprinkle with chives and surround with toasts.

WITH RELISH

In the South and the Midwest, the relish tray traditionally appears on the table with the first course of a festive meal and stays there until dessert. Usually the selection consists of just olives, relishes (of course) and crudités like carrot and celery sticks and radishes, but any of the following suggestions will give yours a bit more panache.

• Offer a variety of intriguing olives, like almond-stuffed green olives, small black Niçois olives, brine-cured Italian olives with herbs, and garlic-stuffed olives.

• Most deli sections in the market have great crunchy bread-and-butter pickles and dill pickles. Also try pickled onions and beets.

• *Giardiniera*, which is available in jars, is a combination of pickled cauliflower, red bell pepper, carrot and celery. Marinated mushrooms and artichokes would also be terrific.

• Specialty foods stores often stock a number of delicious fruit chutneys, many of them with interesting spices that would complement a holiday turkey or ham.

BUTTER BEAN AND CUMIN HUMMUS

Canned butter beans called for here make an exceptionally creamy hummus.

MAKES ABOUT 3 CUPS

2 large garlic cloves
2 15- to 16-ounce cans butter beans, rinsed, drained
⅔ cup tahini (sesame seed paste)*
6 tablespoons fresh lemon juice
¼ cup olive oil (preferably extra-virgin)
1 tablespoon ground cumin
4 tablespoons (about) water

Pita breads, cut into wedges
Assorted cut-up fresh vegetables

Finely chop garlic in processor. Add beans and next 4 ingredients; process until smooth. Mix in water 1 tablespoon at a time, thinning to desired consistency. Season with salt and pepper. Spoon into bowl. (*Can be made 3 days ahead.*

Cover; chill. Bring to room temperature; thin with additional water before serving, if desired.)

Serve with pita bread and vegetables.

*Sold at Middle Eastern markets, natural foods stores and some supermarkets.

TAHINI: SMOOTH SESAME

Tahini is a smooth, thin paste made from crushed roasted sesame seeds. It can vary in color from beige to brown, depending on how long the seeds have been roasted; a darker shade indicates a more robust taste. Tahini is usually used to flavor Middle Eastern dishes like hummus and *baba ghanouj* (a purée that also includes eggplant, olive oil, lemon juice and garlic).

RED CAVIAR DIP

A sophisticated yet simple dip that is wonderful with toast triangles, crackers or some assorted raw vegetables.

MAKES ABOUT 1 CUP

1 cup sour cream
2 green onions, very thinly sliced
1 tablespoon fresh lemon juice
1 tablespoon plus 1 teaspoon chopped fresh chives
¼ cup plus 3 tablespoons salmon caviar, drained, gently rinsed

Mix sour cream, green onions, lemon juice and 1 tablespoon chives in medium bowl. Gently fold in ¼ cup caviar. Transfer to serving bowl. (*Cover and refrigerate at least 6 hours and up to 1 day.*)

Sprinkle dip with remaining 1 teaspoon chives and 3 tablespoons caviar.

CROSTINI WITH GORGONZOLA AND FIGS

The sweet figs and tangy Gorgonzola are perfect partners in this unique and delicious take on a popular hors d'oeuvre.

MAKES 8

8 ⅓-inch-thick baguette slices

⅓ cup crumbled Gorgonzola cheese (about 2 ounces), room temperature
1 tablespoon butter, room temperature
3 large fresh ripe figs, cut into thin wedges
2 teaspoons olive oil (preferably extra-virgin)

Preheat broiler. Arrange baguette slices on baking sheet. Broil until lightly toasted on 1 side.

Mash crumbled Gorgonzola and 1 tablespoon butter in small bowl until smooth. Spread Gorgonzola mixture evenly over untoasted side of baguette slices. Top with figs. Drizzle oil over figs. Broil until Gorgonzola mixture bubbles around edges, about 3 minutes. Transfer crostini to platter and serve.

JUST DUCKY

For a unique hors d'oeuvre, prepare *crostini* with the delicious smoked Muscovy duck from Grimaud Farms (it's also great in salads and quesadillas and on pizza). Call 800-466-9955.

SMOKED SALMON WITH SOUR CREAM-CAPER SAUCE

A simple but elegant cold dish. The sauce can be made a day in advance.

12 TO 14 SERVINGS

1 16-ounce container sour cream
⅔ cup chopped red onion
¼ cup drained capers
2 tablespoons chopped fresh Italian parsley
1 teaspoon ground black pepper

1 whole side of pre-sliced smoked salmon (about 2 pounds)
2 16-ounce loaves cocktail rye and/or pumpernickel bread
Fresh Italian parsley sprigs

Mix sour cream, onion, capers, chopped parsley and pepper in medium bowl. Season to taste with salt. (*Sauce can be made 1 day ahead. Cover and refrigerate.*)

Place salmon on platter. Arrange bread slices around salmon. Garnish with parsley sprigs and serve with sauce.

ARTICHOKE BRUSCHETTA

MAKES 16

1 6-ounce jar marinated artichoke hearts, drained, patted dry, chopped
½ cup grated Romano cheese
⅓ cup finely chopped red onion
5 to 6 tablespoons mayonnaise

16 ⅓-inch-thick French bread baguette rounds

Place first 3 ingredients in bowl. Mix in enough mayonnaise to form thick spread.

Preheat broiler. Top bread rounds with spread. Arrange bruschetta on baking sheet. Broil until spread is heated through and begins to brown, about 2 minutes.

Deviled Eggs with Curry

6 SERVINGS

6 large hard-boiled eggs, shelled
¼ cup mayonnaise
1 tablespoon minced green onion
¾ teaspoon curry powder
1 tablespoon minced fresh parsley
  Niçois olives (optional)*

Cut hard-boiled eggs lengthwise in half. Scoop yolks into medium bowl. Mash yolks with fork. Add mayonnaise, minced green onion and curry powder; mix well. Season yolk mixture to taste with salt and pepper. Divide filling among egg halves, mounding slightly. Arrange eggs on platter. Sprinkle with minced parsley. (*Can be prepared 8 hours ahead. Cover and refrigerate.*) Garnish eggs with Niçois olives, if desired, and serve.

   Niçois olives are small brine-cured black olives available at specialty foods stores and in some supermarkets.

ANY WAY YOU SLICE IT

Quick as a bunny, the "Nerone" egg slicer from Esclusivo cuts hard-boiled eggs into neat thin rounds. Made in Italy of stainless steel and sturdy plastic, it comes in a dozen colors. Call 847-549-9881 to order or for stores.

Belgian Endive with Egg Salad

With the endive leaves arranged in concentric circles on the platter, this is an especially attractive addition to the buffet table.

12 TO 14 SERVINGS

4 hard-boiled eggs, shelled, finely chopped
3 tablespoons mayonnaise
2 tablespoons Dijon mustard
½ teaspoon celery salt

6 heads Belgian endive
4 ounces cooked bay shrimp, well drained
  Paprika

Mix chopped eggs, mayonnaise, mustard and celery salt in medium bowl. (*Can be made 1 day ahead. Cover and refrigerate.*)

   Cut off and discard root ends of endive. Separate leaves. Place 1 generous teaspoon egg mixture at wide end of each leaf. Place 1 shrimp atop each; sprinkle with paprika.

   On large platter, arrange leaves in concentric circles resembling flower. (*Can be made 4 hours ahead. Cover; chill.*)

Smoked Salmon Tartare with Ginger and Sesame

In the early part of the decade, an appreciation of Asian flavors, a desire for spa-style cuisine, and the popularity of sushi dove-tailed with the creation of this appetizer, usually prepared with raw salmon or tuna. The dish is now found on restaurant menus nationwide. This version, which calls for smoked salmon, features a wonderful combination of Pacific Rim flavors.

6 FIRST-COURSE SERVINGS

2 tablespoons fresh lemon juice
1 teaspoon wasabi powder (horseradish powder)*
6 ounces sliced smoked salmon (not lox), finely chopped
¼ cup finely diced seeded peeled English hothouse cucumber
1 tablespoon minced fresh cilantro
1 tablespoon minced green onion
1 tablespoon toasted sesame seeds
1½ teaspoons minced peeled fresh ginger
1 teaspoon oriental sesame oil
2 8x1½-inch strips dried nori (cut from one 8x8-inch sheet)* Water crackers or Japanese rice crackers

Stir lemon juice and wasabi powder in medium bowl to blend. Mix in salmon, cucumber, cilantro, green onion, sesame seeds, ginger and sesame oil. Shape all of salmon mixture into 1½-inch-thick patty, about 3½ inches in diameter. Moisten ends of nori strips. Wrap nori strips snugly around sides of patty, pressing ends together to seal. Place salmon tartare on platter. (Can be made 4 hours ahead. Cover; refrigerate.) Surround with crackers.

*Wasabi powder and nori, thin sheets of dried seaweed, are available at Japanese markets and in the Asian foods section of some supermarkets.

Sugar and Spice Pepitas

Party alert: This spicy snack is perfect with chilled sparkling wine or ice-cold beer.

MAKES 2 CUPS

Nonstick vegetable oil spray
2 cups shelled pepitas
⅓ cup sugar
1 large egg white, beaten until frothy
1 tablespoon chili powder
1 teaspoon ground cinnamon
½ teaspoon salt
¼ teaspoon ground cumin
¼ to ½ teaspoon cayenne pepper

Preheat oven to 350°F. Spray baking sheet with nonstick spray. Mix pepitas and next 6 ingredients in medium bowl. Stir in ¼ teaspoon to ½ teaspoon cayenne pepper, depending on spiciness desired. Spread pepitas in single layer on baking sheet.

Bake until pepitas are golden and

dry, stirring occasionally, about 15 minutes. Remove from oven. Separate pepitas with fork while still warm. Cool.

SMOKED-SALMON PIZZA WITH RED ONION AND DILL

Red onion and fresh dill make nice toppings. Serve the pizza with lemon wedges.

6 APPETIZER SERVINGS

1 10-ounce purchased fully baked
    pizza crust

4 ounces cream cheese, room
    temperature
¼ cup minced red onion
1 tablespoon chopped fresh dill
2 teaspoons grated lemon peel
1 teaspoon prepared white
    horseradish

4 to 6 ounces thinly sliced smoked
    salmon

Preheat oven to 450°F. Place pizza crust on baking sheet. Bake until crisp at edges, about 13 minutes. Transfer crust to rack; cool to lukewarm.

Blend cream cheese with next 4 ingredients. Season with salt and pepper.

Spread cheese topping over crust, leaving 1-inch border. Top with salmon. Slice pizza and transfer to platter.

SCALLOPS AND LEEKS IN STAR ANISE-ORANGE SAUCE

Star anise has been showing up all over restaurant menus lately, even in seafood dishes. This light and lively first course was inspired by such recipes.

4 FIRST-COURSE SERVINGS

1 cup fresh orange juice
4 whole star anise
2 tablespoons sugar
1 teaspoon cornstarch

2 tablespoons peanut oil

1 tablespoon ½x⅛-inch orange
    peel strips (orange part only)
4 medium leeks (white and pale
    green parts only), cut crosswise
    into ½-inch pieces
16 sea scallops

Boil juice and star anise in saucepan until juice is reduced to ⅔ cup, about 4 minutes. Cool; remove star anise and reserve. Whisk sugar and cornstarch into juice.

Heat oil in heavy large skillet over medium-high heat. Add orange peel strips and reserved star anise to skillet and sauté 1 minute. Add leeks; sauté until tender, about 6 minutes. Add scallops; sauté until opaque in center, turning once, about 3 minutes. Add juice mixture; boil until sauce thickens slightly, about 2 minutes. Season with salt and pepper.

THE STAR ANISE OF CHINA

Named (both in English and in Chinese) for its distinctive shape—its Mandarin name, *bah-jyao*, means "eight points"—star anise is the dried fruit of an evergreen tree that is a member of the magnolia family and grows wild in southern China, reaching a height of about 25 feet. The tree starts to bear fruit at about six years of age and can continue to produce over the next one hundred years. In spring, the tree blooms with yellow flowers; from them emerges the brown fruit that assumes a star shape as it ripens, with each point containing a single shiny seed. In cooking, the dried star and seeds can be ground up as seasoning or simmered whole in liquid mixtures to enhance broths and syrups.

BEEF AND BROCCOLI WONTONS WITH GINGER DIPPING SAUCE

Wonton wrappers can be found in the refrigerator section and rice vinegar in the Asian foods section of many supermarkets.

MAKES ABOUT 45

6 tablespoons soy sauce
¼ cup plus 2 teaspoons minced
  peeled fresh ginger
¼ cup rice vinegar
3 tablespoons honey

½ pound lean ground beef
1 cup chopped broccoli florets
¾ cup chopped onion
1 large egg
1½ teaspoons minced garlic
½ teaspoon ground black pepper
½ teaspoon salt
1 12-ounce package wonton
  wrappers
2 tablespoons oriental sesame oil

Blend 4 tablespoons soy sauce, ¼ cup ginger, vinegar and honey in small bowl.

Combine beef and next 6 ingredients in medium bowl. Mix in remaining 2 tablespoons soy sauce and 2 teaspoons ginger. Place several wrappers on work surface; brush edges lightly with water. Place heaping 1 teaspoon beef filling in center of each. Fold wrappers diagonally in half, pressing edges to seal. Place wontons on waxed paper. Repeat with remaining wrappers and filling.

Preheat oven to 250°F. Heat ½ tablespoon oil in heavy large skillet over medium heat; add ¼ of wontons. Fry until wontons are golden and filling is cooked through, about 3 minutes per side. Transfer to baking sheet; keep warm in oven. Repeat frying with remaining wontons, using ½ tablespoon oil per batch. Serve wontons with sauce.

RISOTTO WITH SPICY SAUSAGE

Here's a quick and satisfying starter.

8 FIRST-COURSE SERVINGS

1 pound spicy Italian sausages, casings removed
1½ cups chopped onion
2 large garlic cloves, chopped
1¼ cups medium-grain white rice (such as blue rose)
4 to 5 cups canned low-salt chicken broth
1¼ cups grated Parmesan cheese
½ cup chopped fresh Italian parsley

Sauté sausage, onion and garlic in heavy large saucepan over medium heat until onion is tender, breaking up sausage with spoon, about 8 minutes. Add rice and stir 1 minute. Add 4 cups broth. Reduce heat to medium-low and simmer until broth is absorbed, stirring frequently, about 15 minutes. Continue to simmer until rice is just tender and mixture is creamy, adding more broth ¼ cup at a time and stirring frequently, about 6 minutes longer. Mix in ¼ cup cheese and ¼ cup parsley. Season with salt and pepper.

Transfer risotto to large bowl. Sprinkle with remaining ¼ cup parsley. Pass remaining 1 cup cheese separately.

QUICKER BITES

Pressed for time? Don't overlook the high-quality prepared foods now available at the supermarket. For a pretty presentation, keep it simple: Use decorative plates or bowls, and add fresh herb garnishes.

• Top slices of sourdough baguette with herbed cream cheese and smoked salmon. Garnish with lemon wedges.

• Make an easy antipasto platter by arranging roasted red peppers (sold in jars), marinated artichoke hearts and mushrooms, caponata and olives on a colorful plate. Serve with crusty bread.

• Wrap paper-thin slices of prosciutto around crispy breadsticks.

• Mix equal quantities of mayonnaise and prepared pesto to serve as a dip with packaged, pre-cut raw vegetables.

• Arrange peeled cooked shrimp on a platter. Offer lemon wedges and good-quality bottled cocktail sauce alongside.

Chicken and Mushroom Quesadillas

These quesadillas are cooked on the grill. Serve them with salsa and sour cream.

12 TO 16 SERVINGS

¼ cup (½ stick) butter
2½ teaspoons chili powder
2 garlic cloves, minced
1 teaspoon dried oregano
4 ounces fresh shiitake mushrooms; stemmed, sliced
4 ounces button mushrooms, sliced
1½ cups shredded cooked chicken
⅔ cup finely chopped onion
⅓ cup chopped fresh cilantro
2½ cups grated Monterey Jack cheese

Olive oil
16 5½-inch-diameter corn tortillas

Melt butter in large skillet over medium-high heat. Add chili powder, garlic and oregano. Sauté until fragrant, about 1 minute. Add shiitake and button mushrooms and sauté until tender, about 10 minutes. Remove from heat. Mix in chicken, onion and cilantro. Cool 10 minutes. Mix in cheese. Season with salt and pepper. (*Can be made 8 hours ahead. Cover and chill.*)

Prepare barbecue (medium heat). Lightly brush oil on 1 side of 8 tortillas. Place tortillas, oil side down, on large baking sheet. Divide chicken mixture among tortillas, spreading to even thickness. Top with remaining 8 tortillas; press, then brush with oil.

Grill quesadillas until heated through and golden brown, about 3 minutes per side. Cut into wedges.

Sweet and Spicy Candied Pecans

MAKES 1½ CUPS

Nonstick vegetable oil spray
3 tablespoons light corn syrup
1½ tablespoons sugar
¾ teaspoon salt
¼ teaspoon (generous) freshly ground black pepper
⅛ teaspoon cayenne pepper
1½ cups pecan pieces

Preheat oven to 325°F. Spray baking sheet with nonstick spray. Combine corn syrup and next 4 ingredients in large bowl. Stir to blend. Add pecans; stir gently to coat. Transfer to baking sheet.

Place large piece of foil on work surface. Bake pecans 5 minutes. Using fork, stir pecans to coat with melted spice mixture. Continue baking until pecans are golden and coating bubbles, about 10 minutes. Transfer to foil. Working quickly, separate nuts with fork. Cool. (*Can be made 3 days ahead. Store airtight at room temperature.*)

DEVIL OF A SNACK

Spice up New Year's celebrations with tangy Cocktail Devils from the El Paso Chile Company. For a 16-ounce package of mixed crunchy flatbread crackers, pistachios, pecans and cheddar biscuits, call Williams-Sonoma at 800-541-2233 for store locations or to order.

Beverages

KIR VODKA MARTINIS

Cocktails made a comeback in the nineties. Martinis were often mixed with vodka instead of the traditional gin, and flavored with a variety of liqueurs and juices.

2 SERVINGS

Ice cubes
⅔ cup currant-flavored vodka
2 teaspoons crème de cassis (black currant-flavored liqueur)
2 lemon twists

Fill cocktail shaker with ice. Add vodka; shake to chill thoroughly. Divide vodka between 2 large Martini glasses. Carefully drop 1 teaspoon crème de cassis into each glass (liqueur will sink to bottom). Garnish each Martini with 1 lemon twist.

HOT COCOA WITH COFFEE LIQUEUR

6 SERVINGS

5 cups milk
⅓ cup unsweetened cocoa powder
6 tablespoons sugar
1½ tablespoons instant coffee powder
Pinch of salt
3 ounces semisweet chocolate, chopped
¼ cup coffee liqueur

Bring first 5 ingredients to simmer in heavy large saucepan over medium heat, whisking frequently. Add chocolate; whisk until melted and smooth. Mix in liqueur. Ladle into mugs and serve.

"POPPING" A CHAMPAGNE CORK

First make sure that the Champagne has been stationary for at least a couple of hours. This reduces the volatility of the carbonation, lessening the likelihood of the cork's flying out when the bottle is opened. ("Popping" the cork can be exciting, but it's not proper etiquette.)

To open the bottle, hold the cork in place with one hand, and with the other hand untwist the wire cage that keeps the cork in the bottle. Rest the bottle on your hip, and twist the bottle slowly, while continuing to hold the cork in place. Ease the cork upward, applying gentle pressure to prevent it from popping out, and making sure that the bottle is not pointed at anyone. Beginners should wrap the top of the bottle in a towel to prevent accidents.

MANGO-BOYSENBERRY MIMOSA

Brunch drinks get updated with this take on the traditional duo of orange juice and Champagne. Note that freshly squeezed orange juice is not the best choice here, as its intense taste can overwhelm the other juices. Topping the drink with a boysenberry "floater" creates a vibrant color contrast.

10 SERVINGS

2 cups frozen unsweetened
  boysenberries, thawed
2 tablespoons sugar

3 cups chilled orange juice (do not
  use freshly squeezed)
1½ cups frozen orange-peach-mango
  juice concentrate
1 750-ml bottle of chilled dry
  Champagne
10 small orange slices

Place 10 berries in freezer; reserve for garnish. Purée remaining berries in processor. Strain through sieve over bowl, pressing on solids. Mix in sugar. *(Purée can be made 1 day ahead. Cover and refrigerate.)*

Whisk orange juice and concentrate in pitcher to blend. Mix in Champagne. Divide mimosa among 10 Champagne glasses. Drizzle 1½ teaspoons berry purée over each. Garnish with orange slices and reserved berries.

SOUTHWESTERN BLOODY MARY

Smoky chipotle chilies add a new dimension to the sizzle in these Bloody Marys.

6 SERVINGS

3 cups canned vegetable juice
2 tablespoons fresh lemon juice
1 tablespoon minced fresh cilantro
1 tablespoon Worcestershire sauce
1 teaspoon finely minced seeded
   canned chipotle chilies*
1 teaspoon ground cumin
1 teaspoon sugar
⅔ cup chilled vodka

   Ice cubes
6 celery stalks with leafy tops
6 fresh red chilies, slit

Mix first 7 ingredients in pitcher. Chill mixture until cold, at least 2 hours or overnight. Mix in vodka.

   Fill 6 tall glasses with ice. Pour Bloody Mary mixture over. Garnish with celery and chilies.

   *Chipotle *chilies canned in a spicy tomato sauce, sometimes called adobo, *are available at Latin American markets, specialty foods stores and some supermarkets.*

TISANE TIME

A tisane, pronounced *ti-zahn*, is simply another name for an herbal tea. Unlike regular black and green teas, which come from the leaves of the *Camellia sinensis* plant, tisanes can be made from the leaves, flowers, barks and seeds of many different edible plants. Some popular tisanes are made from chamomile, mint, lemon balm and verbena.

Unlike regular teas, tisanes do not contain caffeine. Because of that, they are known for their calming, therapeutic and possibly healing effects.

FRENCH 75 COCKTAIL

This intoxicating Champagne cocktail was named after a French 75-millimeter gun used in World War I. Many American bartenders claimed to have invented the drink. One recipe, from 1919, called for absinthe, Calvados and gin, but no Champagne. Supposedly, the Champagne version was introduced at Harry's New York Bar in Paris in 1925. Or the cocktail might have originated with American soldiers in Paris, who added gin and liqueur to Champagne to crank up its potency.

6 SERVINGS

6 tablespoons gin
¼ cup Cointreau or triple sec
1¼ teaspoons fresh lemon juice
6 thin strips lemon peel
   (yellow part only)
1 750-ml bottle of chilled brut
   Champagne

Mix first 3 ingredients in measuring cup. Divide among 6 Champagne glasses. Add 1 lemon strip to each. Fill with Champagne.

BLENDED CITRUS GIN FIZZ

This twist on the classic brunch drink gets its flavor from three types of citrus. For large parties, you can prepare several batches a few hours ahead of time and store them in the freezer. Then, before serving, thaw the mixture slightly and whisk to blend.

4 SERVINGS

22 ice cubes
½ cup gin or vodka
½ cup whipping cream
½ cup club soda
¼ cup frozen lemonade concentrate
¼ cup frozen limeade concentrate
3 tablespoons frozen orange juice
    concentrate
3 tablespoons powdered sugar

Ground nutmeg
Lemon- and lime-peel twists
Lemon slices

Place first 8 ingredients in blender; blend until smooth. Pour into 4 glasses. Sprinkle with nutmeg. Garnish with lemon-and lime-peel twists and lemon slices.

MAKING ICED TEA CRYSTAL-CLEAR

You can avoid preparing a cloudy batch of iced tea by brewing it with cold or lukewarm (not hot) water.

The cloudiness is caused by particles in the tea that are more soluble in hot water than in cold. When those particles are dissolved in hot tea, they are clear, but when the tea cools down, the particles become cloudy. If tea is brewed with cold water in the first place, the cloud-causing particles will never be dissolved, and the iced tea will be crystal clear.

To brew clear iced tea, fill a pitcher or jar with cold water, add tea leaves or bags, and cover. Refrigerate the tea for 24 hours, or let it stand in the sun for 4 hours. Remove tea bags, or if using tea leaves, strain the tea through a paper coffee filter; then serve it over ice.

Hot Apple Cider with Ginger and Cardamom

A lovely seasonal treat that's delicious with dessert.

8 SERVINGS

1 lemon
¼ cup sugar
6 quarter-size pieces crystallized ginger, coarsely chopped
20 cardamom pods
15 whole cloves
2 cinnamon sticks, each broken in half
8 cups unfiltered apple cider

Using vegetable peeler, remove peel (yellow part only) in strips from lemon. Heat heavy large pot over medium heat. Add lemon peel, sugar, ginger, cardamom, cloves and cinnamon and stir until fragrant, about 2 minutes. Add cider and bring to boil. Reduce heat to low and simmer mixture 15 minutes. Strain into mugs and serve.

Candy Cane Hot White Chocolate

Peppermint schnapps makes this drink a candy cane with a kick, but the liquor can be omitted. Either way, indulge and top the hot chocolate with whipped cream and more crushed peppermint candy.

12 SERVINGS

12 cups milk
9 ounces good-quality white chocolate (such as Lindt or Baker's), chopped
1 cup crushed red-and-white-striped candy canes or hard peppermint candies
¼ teaspoon salt
1½ cups peppermint schnapps (optional)
Whipped cream
Additional crushed red-and-white-striped candy canes or hard peppermint candies

Bring milk to simmer in heavy large saucepan. Reduce heat to medium-low. Add white chocolate, 1 cup candy and salt; whisk until smooth. Add schnapps, if desired. Ladle hot chocolate into mugs, dividing equally. Top with whipped cream and additional candy.

PERKING UP THE DAILY GRIND

People in the San Francisco Bay Area have been waking up to their beloved Peet's coffee since 1966. But folks all over can get Peet's rich blends by mail. Call 800-999-2132.

Soups & Salads

Soups and salads take almost no time to prepare. Making soup usually means little more than simmering together a handful of ingredients and seasonings. The result: sensational first courses like Creamy Zucchini Soup or Quick Black Bean Soup. For a great salad, grab prepackaged greens from the market or cook pasta al dente; add a few embellishments; and top with a swiftly whisked dressing. Then present refreshing creations like Salad Bar Cobb or Spicy Asian-Style Pasta Salad.

Soups

CREAMY ZUCCHINI SOUP

Nutmeg adds nice flavor to this soup.

4 SERVINGS

1½ pounds zucchini, cut into ½-inch pieces
1½ cups canned low-salt chicken broth or water
¼ cup whipping cream
¼ teaspoon ground nutmeg
1 tablespoon grated Parmesan cheese

Bring zucchini and broth to boil in heavy medium saucepan. Reduce heat to medium-low, cover and simmer until zucchini is very tender, about 15 minutes.

Working in batches, purée soup in blender until almost smooth. Return soup to same saucepan. Add cream, nutmeg and cheese; stir over medium heat until warm. Season with salt and pepper.

HOW IS A BISQUE DIFFERENT FROM PLAIN OLD SOUP?

Traditionally, a bisque is a thick soup or purée made with shellfish and cream, and thickened with rice, breadcrumbs or a roux. In an authentic bisque, the shells are sometimes used to make a flavorful broth, and brandy, Sherry or white wine is often added for flavor. Nowadays, the word *bisque* can be used to describe just about any cream-based thickened soup prepared with shellfish or with tomatoes or other vegetables.

QUICK BLACK BEAN SOUP

Top with sour cream and chopped cilantro.

6 SERVINGS

2 tablespoons olive oil
1¼ cups chopped onion
4 large garlic cloves, chopped
1 tablespoon chopped fresh thyme or 1½ teaspoons dried
3 15-ounce cans black beans, drained, 1 cup liquid reserved
2 14½-ounce cans low-salt chicken broth
1 28-ounce can diced tomatoes in juice
2 teaspoons ground cumin
1½ teaspoons hot pepper sauce

Heat oil in large pot over medium heat. Add onion, garlic and thyme; sauté until onion is golden, about 8 minutes. Add beans, reserved 1 cup bean liquid, broth, tomatoes with juices, cumin and hot pepper sauce. Bring soup to boil. Reduce heat to medium-low and simmer until flavors blend and soup thickens slightly, stirring occasionally, about 20 minutes.

Working in 2 batches, purée 2½ cups soup in blender until smooth. Mix purée back into soup in pot. Season with salt and pepper. Ladle soup into bowls.

Zucchini and Dill Soup

There's no cream in this rich-tasting soup, so go ahead and garnish it with sour cream. Serve with Bacon and Thyme Biscuits (see page 86).

6 SERVINGS

2 tablespoons (¼ stick) butter
5 zucchini (about 1¼ pounds), thinly sliced
1 large onion, chopped
2 garlic cloves, chopped
1 tablespoon chopped fresh dill
4 cups canned low-salt chicken broth

Melt butter in large pot over medium-high heat. Add next 4 ingredients and sauté until tender, about 10 minutes. Add broth and bring soup to boil. Reduce heat and simmer soup for 10 minutes.

Working in batches, purée soup in blender. Return soup to pot. Season with salt and pepper. (*Can be made 1 day ahead. Cover; chill.*) Bring soup to simmer. Ladle into bowls. Top with sour cream, if desired. Sprinkle with additional dill.

AUSTRIAN IMPORT

Roasted pumpkin seed oil from Austria, where it is a specialty, is delightful swirled into soups or drizzled onto salads. For a 17-ounce bottle from The Grateful Palate, call 888-472-5283.

Appetizer & Side Dish Salads

CONFETTI SALAD WITH RANCH DRESSING

6 SERVINGS

1 English hothouse cucumber, chopped
1 16-ounce bag frozen petite peas, thawed
2 bunches radishes, chopped
1 cup chopped celery
½ cup finely chopped red onion
Ranch Dressing (see recipe)

Combine all vegetables in large bowl. (*Can be prepared 4 hours ahead. Cover and refrigerate.*) Toss salad with enough Ranch Dressing to coat. Season to taste with salt and pepper and serve.

RANCH DRESSING

MAKES 1½ CUPS

¾ cup mayonnaise
½ cup buttermilk
2 tablespoons powdered cultured
   buttermilk blend*
2 tablespoons finely chopped fresh
   parsley
2 tablespoons finely chopped celery
   leaves
1½ teaspoons fresh lemon juice
1½ teaspoons Dijon mustard
¾ teaspoon onion powder
¼ teaspoon dried dillweed

Whisk first 3 ingredients in large bowl. Mix in remaining ingredients. Cover and chill at least 1 hour to blend flavors. *(Dressing can be prepared 5 days ahead. Keep refrigerated.)*
Available alongside the canned and powdered milk in most supermarkets.

WARM SPINACH SALAD WITH PARMESAN TOASTS

Eating your spinach (and radicchio) has never been more pleasant.

6 SERVINGS

2 6-ounce packages fresh baby
   spinach
1 small head radicchio, thinly sliced
⅓ cup extra-virgin olive oil
¼ cup balsamic vinegar
¼ cup dry red wine
1 shallot, minced
½ cup pine nuts, toasted
   Parmesan Toasts (see recipe)

Combine spinach and radicchio in large bowl. Bring oil, vinegar, wine and shallot to simmer in large saucepan. Season with salt and pepper. Immediately pour dressing over salad. Cover with foil and let stand 5 minutes. Toss salad to coat. Divide among plates. Sprinkle with nuts and serve with warm toasts.

PARMESAN TOASTS

MAKES ABOUT 20

1 French-bread baguette
¼ cup (½ stick) butter
⅓ cup extra-virgin olive oil
1 garlic clove, pressed
¾ cup (packed) freshly grated
   Parmesan (about 2½ ounces)

Preheat oven to 350°F. Slice baguette on sharp diagonal to make about twenty 6- to 7-inch-long, ¼-inch-thick slices. Melt butter with oil and garlic in small saucepan over medium heat. Remove from heat. Brush butter mixture over both sides of bread slices. Arrange bread in single layer on 2 baking sheets. Sprinkle cheese over bread. Sprinkle with salt and pepper. Bake until bread is crisp, about 13 minutes. *(Can be made 1 day ahead. Store airtight at room temperature. Rewarm in 350°F oven 3 minutes.)*

WINTER GREENS WITH GRAPEFRUIT VINAIGRETTE

Arugula's bold flavor and the texture of curly frisée team up in this simple salad.

4 SERVINGS

- **2 tablespoons freshly squeezed grapefruit juice**
- **1 tablespoon white wine vinegar**
- **¼ cup olive oil (preferably extra-virgin)**
- **4 cups fresh arugula**
- **4 cups bite-size pieces of frisée* or chicory**

Whisk grapefruit juice and vinegar in large bowl. Whisk in oil. Season vinaigrette to taste with salt and pepper. Add arugula and frisée. Toss greens to coat with vinaigrette. Serve immediately.

A type of endive with curly yellowishgreen leaves; also known as chicorée frisée. Available in the produce section of some specialty foods stores and supermarkets.

MUSHROOM, SQUASH AND BELL PEPPER SALAD

When the weather permits, grill the vegetables on the barbecue.

4 TO 6 SERVINGS

- **½ cup olive oil**
- **¼ cup balsamic vinegar or red wine vinegar**
- **1 tablespoon chopped fresh oregano or 1 teaspoon dried**
- **1 tablespoon chopped fresh thyme or 1 teaspoon dried**
- **1 pound large mushrooms (about 16), stems trimmed**
- **4 medium zucchini, trimmed, cut on diagonal into ½-inch-thick slices**
- **4 yellow crookneck squash, trimmed, cut on diagonal into ½-inch-thick slices**
- **1 large red bell pepper, cut into 2-inch squares**

Whisk oil, vinegar and herbs in small bowl to blend. Season with salt and pepper. Transfer ¼ cup dressing to medium bowl; add mushrooms and toss to coat. Transfer ¼ cup dressing to large bowl; add zucchini, yellow squash and bell pepper and toss to coat.

Preheat broiler. Arrange vegetables on broiler pan. Cook until crisp-tender, about 3 minutes per side. Transfer vegetables to platter. Sprinkle with salt, pepper and remaining dressing. Serve warm or at room temperature.

SPINACH, PEAR AND GREEN BEAN SALAD WITH RIESLING DRESSING

Riesling gives the dressing a delicate flavor. Crumbled blue cheese and toasted walnuts are sharp-crunchy contrasts with appeal.

6 SERVINGS

½ cup diced peeled cored ripe
   Bartlett pear
6 tablespoons medium-dry Riesling
3 tablespoons fresh lemon juice
1 tablespoon chopped shallot
1 teaspoon Dijon mustard
½ cup vegetable oil

½ pound haricots verts or small
   green beans, trimmed

6 cups (packed) baby spinach
   leaves (about 6 ounces)
3 ripe Bartlett pears, quartered,
   cored, cut into ¼-inch-thick slices
¾ cup crumbled blue cheese
¾ cup walnuts, toasted

Purée diced pear, Riesling, lemon juice, shallot and Dijon mustard in food processor until smooth. With machine still running, gradually add vegetable oil through feed tube and blend mixture until smooth. Transfer to bowl. Season dressing to taste with salt and pepper.

Cook green beans in large pot of boiling salted water until just tender but still firm to bite. Drain well. Transfer beans to medium bowl filled with ice water and cool thoroughly. Drain well. *(Dressing and beans can be prepared 1 day ahead. Cover separately and refrigerate.)*

Toss green beans, spinach and sliced pears in large bowl with enough Riesling dressing to coat. Divide salad among plates. Sprinkle with crumbled blue cheese and toasted walnuts.

HOW TO CHECK OIL FOR SPOILAGE

Smell it, and if you're still not sure, taste it. Oil that is spoiled (rancid) will have a strong aroma reminiscent of plastic or petroleum, and a similar—but even stronger—flavor. Be sure to check your oil before each use; even a small amount of rancid oil can ruin an entire dish.

Heat, light, water and oxygen can all turn oil rancid. The best way to store oil is in an airtight container in a cool, dark place. Oil may be kept in the refrigerator, but it will solidify slightly when chilled, and will need to be left at room temperature for an hour or so before it can be poured easily. Also, because contact with water can cause rancidity, be careful not to allow any condensation from the refrigerator or the bottle to come in contact with the oil. Shelf life will vary, depending on the type of oil and how it is stored.

Tomatoes and Feta Cheese with Herb-and-Garlic Dressing

Tomatoes from the garden are put to good use in this salad.

4 SERVINGS

6 tablespoons tarragon vinegar
2 tablespoons chopped fresh oregano or 2 teaspoons dried
1 tablespoon coarse-grained Dijon mustard
1 shallot, minced
1 large garlic clove, minced
1 teaspoon minced peeled fresh ginger
1 cup olive oil

4 large tomatoes, thinly sliced
⅓ cup Kalamata olives or other brine-cured black olives, pitted, chopped
⅓ cup crumbled feta cheese

Combine first 6 ingredients in medium bowl; gradually whisk in oil. Season dressing to taste with salt and pepper.

Arrange tomatoes on platter. Sprinkle with olives and cheese. Drizzle with enough dressing to coat. Serve, passing remaining dressing separately.

Broiled Fennel and Red Bell Pepper Salad

Crumbled feta cheese makes a nice topping.

4 TO 6 SERVINGS

6 tablespoons olive oil
2 large fennel bulbs, tops trimmed, fronds reserved

2 medium red bell peppers, seeded, each cut into 8 strips

2 tablespoons fresh lemon juice

Preheat broiler. Line small baking sheet with foil; brush foil with 1 tablespoon oil. Cut each fennel bulb vertically into 8 wedges, keeping part of core attached to each wedge. Place fennel, cut side down, on prepared sheet. Brush fennel all over with 1½ tablespoons oil. Sprinkle with salt and pepper. Broil fennel until just tender and beginning to brown, turning occasionally, about 10 minutes. Arrange fennel on large serving platter. Set baking sheet aside.

Place bell pepper strips in medium bowl. Add 1½ tablespoons olive oil to the peppers and toss to coat. Arrange peppers on reserved baking sheet. Sprinkle with salt and pepper. Broil until peppers are charred in spots and just tender, turning occasionally, about 10 minutes. Arrange peppers among fennel wedges on platter.

Whisk remaining 2 tablespoons oil and lemon juice in small bowl to blend. Season dressing to taste with salt and pepper. Drizzle dressing over broiled vegetables. Garnish salad with some reserved fennel fronds. Serve salad warm or at room temperature.

SALADS IN A SNAP

So you love the idea of a sophisticated first course, but you can't imagine having the time to prepare one? Well, with the help of some handy purchased ingredients like bagged salad greens and bottled dressings, you can put together a lovely starter in practically no time at all.

• Toss butter lettuce with a vinaigrette, capers and sliced olives, then top with purchased cooked shrimp.

• Drizzle canned julienne of beets with balsamic vinaigrette, and top with crumbled goat cheese and toasted walnuts.

• Dress watercress with fresh lemon juice and olive oil; then arrange prosciutto and some sliced ripe pears on top.

• Sauté chopped bacon, and add some of the drippings to a simple vinaigrette. Toss the dressing with fresh spinach leaves and a few sliced hard-boiled eggs; then sprinkle each serving with the chopped bacon.

• Arugula with a balsamic vinaigrette, sliced purchased roasted bell peppers (packed in jars) and sliced canned hearts of palm make a colorful start to the feast.

ENDIVE AND PEAR SALAD WITH GORGONZOLA CREAM DRESSING

6 SERVINGS

4 tablespoons apple cider vinegar
3 tablespoons olive oil
1 tablespoon honey
4 large heads Belgian endive, sliced
1 large pear, halved, cored, sliced
⅓ cup sour cream
⅓ cup plain yogurt
1¼ cups crumbled Gorgonzola cheese

½ cup hazelnuts, toasted, husked
Chopped fresh chives

Whisk 3 tablespoons vinegar, oil and honey in large bowl to blend. Add endive and pear and toss to coat. Blend sour cream, yogurt and remaining 1 tablespoon vinegar in medium bowl; mix in cheese. Season dressing to taste with salt and pepper.

Mound pear salad on platter. Top with dressing, then nuts and chives.

French Potato Salad

Dijon mustard and dry white wine add French flair to this longtime favorite.

6 SERVINGS

½ cup white wine vinegar
¼ cup Dijon mustard
½ cup olive oil
2 tablespoons chopped fresh parsley
1 tablespoon poppy seeds
1 tablespoon finely chopped shallot

3 pounds small red-skinned potatoes, cut into ¼-inch-thick rounds
¼ cup canned low-salt chicken broth
¼ cup dry white wine

Whisk vinegar and mustard in medium bowl to blend. Gradually whisk in oil. Stir in parsley, poppy seeds and shallot. Season vinaigrette to taste with salt and pepper. (*Can be prepared 1 day ahead. Cover and refrigerate. Bring to room temperature and rewhisk before using.*)

Steam potatoes until tender, about 8 minutes. Transfer to large bowl. Mix in broth and wine. Let stand 5 minutes. Pour vinaigrette over warm potatoes. Toss gently. Season with salt and pepper. Serve warm or at room temperature.

Apple, Endive and Parmesan Salad with Walnut Vinaigrette

6 SERVINGS

4 tablespoons orange juice
2 teaspoons Dijon mustard
¼ cup olive oil
2 tablespoons walnut oil or olive oil
2 Red Delicious or Pippin apples, unpeeled, cored, thinly sliced

4 heads Belgian endive
1 head butter lettuce, torn into bite-size pieces
¾ cup walnuts, toasted, chopped

2 tablespoons chopped chives
Parmesan cheese shavings

Whisk 2 tablespoons orange juice and mustard in small bowl to blend. Whisk in olive oil and walnut oil. Season dressing to taste with salt and pepper. Toss apple slices and remaining 2 tablespoons orange juice in large bowl.

Separate endive leaves; set aside 24 leaves. Slice remaining leaves. Add sliced endive, lettuce and walnuts to bowl with apples. Add dressing; toss to coat.

Arrange 4 reserved endive leaves in spoke fashion on each of 6 plates. Mound salad atop leaves. Sprinkle with chives. Top each with Parmesan shavings.

Hearts of Palm Salad with Olives and Ham

Nice as an appetizer or a simple lunch.

4 TO 6 SERVINGS

1 tablespoon fresh lemon juice
1 tablespoon white wine vinegar
3 garlic cloves, chopped
1½ teaspoons dried oregano
6 tablespoons olive oil

2 14-ounce cans hearts of palm,
  drained, rinsed
6 ounces ham, cut into matchstick-
  size strips (about 1½ cups)
1 cup assorted olives, pitted, sliced

Lettuce leaves

Combine first 4 ingredients in small bowl. Gradually whisk in oil. Season dressing to taste with salt and pepper.

Cut hearts of palm on diagonal into ½-inch-thick slices. Place in large bowl. Add ham and olives. Toss with enough dressing to coat generously.

Arrange lettuce leaves on plates. Spoon salad atop lettuce and serve.

ARTICHOKE, LIMA BEAN AND PEA SALAD

10 SERVINGS

¼ cup red wine vinegar
2 tablespoons minced shallot
2 tablespoons whipping cream
¼ cup extra-virgin olive oil

2 14½-ounce cans chicken broth
1 16-ounce bag frozen baby lima
  beans
2 14-ounce cans water-packed
  artichoke hearts, drained,
  quartered
1 16-ounce bag frozen petite peas

¼ cup chopped fresh mint
  Fresh mint sprigs

Whisk vinegar, shallot and cream in small bowl. Gradually whisk in oil. Season vinaigrette with salt and pepper.

Bring chicken broth to simmer in large saucepan. Add lima beans. Cover and simmer until tender, about 10 min-utes. Using slotted spoon, transfer beans to large bowl. Add artichoke hearts to broth. Cook 2 minutes. Add peas. Cover and cook until peas and artichokes are heated through, about 3 minutes longer. Drain well. Add to beans.

Add chopped mint to vegetables. Mix in enough vinaigrette to coat. Season with salt and pepper. Garnish with mint sprigs. Serve warm or at room temperature.

COUNTRY BEET SALAD

4 TO 6 SERVINGS

½ cup olive oil
3 tablespoons white wine vinegar
1 15-ounce can baby beets, drained,
  cut into ½-inch pieces

4 slices bacon, chopped
4 cups 1-inch cubes French bread
1 4½-ounce package mixed greens
2 hard-boiled eggs, shelled, diced
¼ cup pine nuts, toasted

Whisk oil and vinegar in small bowl to blend. Season dressing with salt and pepper. Place beets in medium bowl; mix in 2 tablespoons dressing. Sauté bacon in heavy large skillet over medium heat until crisp. Using slotted spoon, transfer bacon to paper towels and drain. Whisk 1 tablespoon bacon drippings into dressing. Add bread to remaining drippings in skillet and sauté until crisp, about 6 minutes. Place croutons in large bowl. Add greens, eggs, pine nuts, beets and bacon. Toss with enough dressing to coat.

SPICY SESAME AND GINGER NOODLE SALAD

You can make the noodle salad and the dressing a day ahead, and then toss them together before serving.

14 SERVINGS

¾ cup low-sodium soy sauce
9 tablespoons fresh lemon juice
6 tablespoons minced peeled
   fresh ginger

6 tablespoons tahini (sesame seed paste)*
4¼ tablespoons honey
2 teaspoons dried crushed red pepper
6 tablespoons oriental sesame oil

3 8-ounce packages chuka soba (thin yellow Japanese noodles)**
6 medium carrots, peeled, cut into matchstick-size strips
1½ cucumbers, peeled, seeded, cut into matchstick-size strips
1½ bunches green onions, thinly sliced diagonally
12 ounces snow peas, trimmed, thinly sliced diagonally
3 red bell peppers, cut into matchstick-size strips
¼ cup sesame seeds, toasted

Whisk first 6 ingredients in medium bowl. Mix in 3 tablespoons sesame oil.

Cook noodles in large pot of boiling salted water until just tender but still firm to bite, stirring occasionally, about 5 minutes. Drain. Transfer hot noodles to large bowl. Toss with 3 tablespoons oil. Add all vegetables; toss. *(Salad and dressing can be made 1 day ahead. Chill separately.)* Toss with dressing; season with salt and pepper. Sprinkle with sesame seeds.

*Available at Middle Eastern and natural foods stores and some supermarkets.

**Available at Asian markets and some supermarkets.

WALDORF SALAD

This simple apple salad got its name from the luxurious Waldorf-Astoria Hotel in New York. Invented in 1896 not by a chef but by the maître d'hôtel Oscar Tschirky, the Waldorf salad was an instant success. As often happens, many variations evolved—some with raisins, some with chopped nuts. This one has green apples and red seedless grapes.

6 SERVINGS

⅔ cup dried tart cherries*

1 cup boiling water

½ cup mayonnaise
3 tablespoons sour cream
2 tablespoons fresh lemon juice
1 teaspoon sugar
4 Granny Smith apples, cored,
  cut into ½-inch cubes
1⅓ cups very thinly sliced celery
1⅓ cups red seedless grapes, halved

Romaine lettuce leaves
Sweet and Spicy Candied Pecans
(see page 13)

Soak cherries in 1 cup boiling water until softened, about 10 minutes. Drain.

Whisk mayonnaise and next 3 ingredients in large bowl. Add apples, celery, grapes and cherries; toss. Season with salt and pepper.

Arrange lettuce on platter. Spoon salad over. Top salad with candied pecans.

Sold at specialty foods stores, natural foods stores and some supermarkets.

SPICY ASIAN-STYLE PASTA SALAD

Serve this as a side dish, or add some cooked shrimp or chicken for a main course. Look for the sesame oil in the Asian foods section of the supermarket.

6 SERVINGS

1 pound linguine, broken in half

4 tablespoons oriental sesame oil
3 tablespoons honey
3 tablespoons soy sauce
3 tablespoons balsamic vinegar
¼ teaspoon cayenne pepper

3 red bell peppers, seeded,
  thinly sliced
3 cups snow peas
1 large red onion, thinly sliced
¾ cup honey-roasted peanuts,
  coarsely chopped
½ cup chopped fresh basil

Cook pasta in large pot of boiling salted water until tender but still firm to bite, stirring occasionally. Drain very well. Transfer to large bowl.

Whisk 3 tablespoons sesame oil, honey, soy sauce, vinegar and cayenne pepper in small bowl to blend. Season with salt. Mix half of dressing into pasta.

Heat remaining 1 tablespoon oil in heavy large pot over medium-high heat. Add bell peppers, peas and onion and sauté until just beginning to wilt, about 2 minutes. Add vegetables to pasta. Mix in peanuts, basil and enough dressing to coat. Serve, passing any remaining dressing separately.

SPICY-SWEET PEANUT DRESSING

Serve this Thai-style dressing over chilled pasta or mixed raw vegetables.

MAKES ABOUT 2½ CUPS

1 cup smooth old-fashioned peanut
  butter
½ cup freshly brewed black tea,
  room temperature

½ cup orange juice
3 tablespoons oriental sesame oil
3 tablespoons honey
2 tablespoons soy sauce
2 tablespoons rice vinegar
1 tablespoon minced peeled fresh ginger
2 teaspoons grated orange peel
3 garlic cloves, minced
1½ teaspoons minced canned chipotle chilies*

Mix all ingredients in medium bowl. Stir until mixture is blended and smooth.

*Chipotle *chilies canned in a spicy tomato sauce, sometimes called* adobo, *are available at Latin American markets, specialty foods stores and some supermarkets.*

Modern Macaroni Salad

The pickles add crunch and tangy flavor to an old-time favorite.

6 TO 8 SERVINGS

2⅓ cups elbow macaroni (about 10 ounces)

⅔ cup mayonnaise
¼ cup Dijon mustard
2 tablespoons fresh lemon juice
1½ tablespoons sugar
1⅓ cups chopped drained bread-and-butter pickles
1¼ cups chopped celery
2 4-ounce jars sliced pimientos, drained
½ cup thinly sliced green onions

Cook macaroni in large pot of boiling salted water just until tender but still firm to bite, stirring occasionally. Drain. Rinse under cold water; drain well.

Whisk mayonnaise, mustard, lemon juice and sugar in large bowl. Mix in macaroni, pickles, celery, pimientos and onions. Season with salt and pepper.

A PERFECTLY PROPORTIONED VINAIGRETTE

The proportions for a classic vinaigrette are three parts oil to one part vinegar. A generous seasoning with salt and pepper is also included in the traditional recipe.

There is some controversy over whether vinaigrette must contain vinegar to earn the name. According to *Larousse Gastronomique,* the definitive French-food encyclopedia, if the vinegar is replaced by lemon juice, the dressing may still be called vinaigrette. (The proportions change, however, to half oil, half lemon juice.)

These days, many people prefer a lighter mixture and may use half oil and half vinegar, adding a bit of sugar to cut the tartness. Another trick to use when increasing the amount of vinegar is to substitute balsamic vinegar, which isn't quite as strong as regular vinegar.

Here's a tip from *Larousse:* Salt does not dissolve well in oil, so mix the salt with the vinegar first, then add the oil and the pepper.

SMOKED TROUT, WATERCRESS AND APPLE SALAD WITH CREAMY HORSERADISH DRESSING

An elegant salad that would add a sophisticated touch to any festive menu.

6 SERVINGS

1 cup whipping cream
⅓ cup prepared horseradish
4 tablespoons olive oil
2 tablespoons plus 2 teaspoons
   apple cider vinegar
2 teaspoons finely chopped
   fresh dill
⅛ teaspoon cayenne pepper

6 cups trimmed watercress sprigs
   (about 2 large bunches)
½ cup very thinly sliced red onion
2 red apples, cored, thinly sliced
9 ounces smoked trout or smoked
   whitefish chubs,* coarsely flaked
   Fresh dill sprigs (optional)

Whisk cream, horseradish, 2 tablespoons oil, 2 tablespoons vinegar, chopped dill and cayenne in small bowl to blend. Season to taste with salt and pepper.

Place watercress in large bowl. Add ⅓ cup cream dressing, 2 tablespoons oil and 2 teaspoons vinegar and toss to coat. Season to taste with salt and pepper. Mound watercress in center of each of 6 plates. Top with sliced onion. Fan apple slices atop salad. Top with trout. Spoon dressing over. Garnish with dill sprigs, if desired, and serve.

*Smoked trout and smoked whitefish chubs are available at specialty foods stores and at some delicatessens and supermarkets.

ZINFANDEL SALAD DRESSING

A nice dressing for greens or coleslaw.

MAKES ABOUT 1¼ CUPS

⅓ cup sliced green onions
¼ cup red Zinfandel wine
3 tablespoons red wine vinegar
2 garlic cloves
½ teaspoon salt
½ teaspoon ground black pepper
¾ cup mayonnaise

Combine all ingredients except mayonnaise in blender; blend until onions and garlic are minced. Add mayonnaise and blend until smooth. Refrigerate until cold. Whisk dressing before using.

Main-Course Salads

SALAD BAR COBB

Cobb salad was created at the Brown Derby, which opened in Los Angeles in 1926. Owner Robert Cobb placed diced vegetables, chicken and cheese on a bed of greens, and topped it all with his French dressing. Most of the ingredients for this recipe can be found at supermarket salad bars.

6 SERVINGS

½ cup extra-virgin olive oil
3 tablespoons red wine vinegar
1 tablespoon chopped fresh chives
2 teaspoons honey-Dijon mustard
2 teaspoons Worcestershire sauce

2 4½-ounce packages baby greens
2 cups diced smoked turkey or chicken (about 10 ounces)
2 cups diced plum tomatoes
1½ cups diced avocados
1 cup chopped peeled hard-boiled eggs
1 cup crumbled cooked bacon
1 cup crumbled blue cheese

Blend first 5 ingredients in small bowl. Season dressing with salt and pepper.

Divide greens among 6 plates. Place rows of turkey, tomatoes and avocados atop greens. Sprinkle each salad with eggs, bacon and blue cheese. Drizzle salads with dressing and serve.

SOUTHWESTERN CHICKEN AND PASTA SALAD

Pick up a rotisserie chicken at the market, or use leftovers to keep the preparation easy.

8 SERVINGS

1 pound farfalle (bow-tie) pasta

4 tablespoons olive oil
2 cups diced cooked chicken
8 green onions, chopped
6 plum tomatoes, chopped
1 15-ounce can golden hominy, drained
1 15-ounce can black beans, drained
1 12-ounce bottle mild green taco sauce
1 cup chopped fresh cilantro

Cook pasta in large pot of boiling salted water until tender but still firm to bite. Drain; rinse under cold running water and drain again.

Transfer pasta to large bowl. Add oil and toss to coat. Mix in chicken, green onions, tomatoes, hominy, beans, taco sauce and cilantro. Season salad generously with salt and pepper.

CRAB SALAD WITH SUN-DRIED TOMATO LOUIS DRESSING

It's unclear just who the Louis of Crab Louis salad fame was; perhaps he was affiliated with the Olympic Club in Seattle, where opera star Enrico Caruso, who visited there in 1904, is said to have fallen in love with the crab salad. San Francisco also claims the dish, which reached its zenith there in the teens, as a specialty at Solari's restaurant and at the St. Francis Hotel.

4 TO 6 SERVINGS

1¼ cups mayonnaise
⅓ cup finely chopped drained
  oil-packed sun-dried tomatoes
¼ cup milk
1½ tablespoons chopped fresh chives
1½ tablespoons chopped fresh parsley
1 tablespoon fresh lemon juice
1½ teaspoons tomato paste
¼ teaspoon Worcestershire sauce
¼ teaspoon hot pepper sauce

1 pound asparagus, trimmed to
  5-inch lengths

12 cups lightly packed bite-size
  pieces romaine lettuce
  (from 2 heads)
1 pound lump crabmeat
1 cup cherry tomatoes
2 large hard-boiled eggs, cut into
  wedges
  Lemon wedges

Whisk first 9 ingredients in medium bowl to blend. Season dressing to taste with salt and pepper.

Cook asparagus in saucepan of boiling salted water until crisp-tender, about 3 minutes. Drain. Transfer to bowl of ice water; cool. Drain. *(Dressing and asparagus can be made 1 day ahead. Cover; chill.)*

Place lettuce in large bowl. Toss with enough dressing to coat. Mound lettuce on plates. Top with crab. Garnish with asparagus, tomatoes, eggs and lemon. Pass remaining dressing separately.

Main Courses

The secret behind quick main courses is to think small,
concentrating on bite-sized or individually
proportioned ingredients that cook in minutes,
leaving you with more time to attend to such
details as seasonings, sauces and garnishes.
This selection of recipes, from Sautéed
Shrimp with Lemon-Garlic Butter to
Cornmeal-Crusted Chicken Breasts,
from Beef Medallions with Cognac
Sauce to Fettuccine Quatro
Formaggi, proves just how
successful that approach can be.

Seafood

SEARED TUNA PEPPER STEAKS

A spicy pepper coating and an Asian-style sauce give these tuna steaks an intense flavor. Serve mashed or oven-roasted sweet potatoes alongside. Look for the sesame oil in the Asian foods section of the supermarket.

4 SERVINGS

- 4 6- to 7-ounce ahi tuna steaks (each about 1 inch thick)
- 1 tablespoon coarsely cracked black pepper
- 2 teaspoons oriental sesame oil
- 2 tablespoons soy sauce
- ¼ cup dry Sherry
- 2 tablespoons chopped fresh chives or green onion tops

Sprinkle tuna steaks on both sides with salt, then sprinkle with coarsely cracked black pepper, pressing gently to adhere. Heat sesame oil in large nonstick skillet over high heat. Add tuna steaks and sear until brown outside and just opaque in center, about 3 minutes per side. Using tongs, transfer tuna steaks to platter. Tent platter loosely with foil to keep tuna steaks warm. Add soy sauce, then Sherry to same skillet. Reduce heat and simmer until mixture is slightly reduced, scraping up any browned bits, about 1 minute. Spoon sauce over tuna steaks. Sprinkle with chives or green onion tops.

THE PEPPER SPECTRUM

There are five peppercorn types available: green, black, white, pink and Szechuan. Green, black and white peppercorns come from the same plant, but are picked at different stages of ripeness.

Green peppercorns are picked while still under-ripe. They are usually packaged in jars filled with brine or vinegar but are also sold dried. Their mild flavor is nice in sauces for red meat, duck and game.

Black peppercorns are picked when they are half ripe. They are sold dried, and they are almost always used ground because they have the strongest flavor.

White peppercorns are completely ripe. Solid red when harvested, they are soaked in brine, and then the outer red shells are removed. The white peppercorns that remain are then dried. Many people favor ground white pepper in cream sauces or clear broths because it does not color the dish.

Pink peppercorns are the dried berries of a particular rose bush. They have a somewhat bitter flavor, and are good used whole in sauces for game, fish and poultry, or ground and pressed into cheeses like Brie and chèvre.

Szechuan peppercorns are the dried red berries of an ash tree. They have an unusual numbing taste and are used widely in Asian cooking, especially in the spicy Szechuan and Hunan cuisines of China.

Sea Bass with Shallots, Garlic and Marsala

4 SERVINGS

3 tablespoons olive oil
6 large shallots, thinly sliced
3 large garlic cloves, thinly sliced
¼ teaspoon (generous) dried
  crushed red pepper
4 6- to 8-ounce sea bass fillets

⅓ cup dry Marsala
⅓ cup bottled clam juice
1 teaspoon white wine vinegar
  Toasted pine nuts

Preheat oven to 400°F. Heat oil in heavy large ovenproof skillet over medium-high heat. Add shallots, garlic and crushed red pepper and sauté until shallots soften, about 3 minutes. Remove from heat. Let stand 5 minutes. Sprinkle fish with salt and pepper. Add fish to skillet; turn to coat with shallot mixture. Roast fish in oven until just opaque in center, about 10 minutes. Transfer fish to platter; tent loosely with foil to keep warm.

Using oven mitt to hold handle, set skillet over medium-high heat. Add Marsala, clam juice and vinegar and boil until sauce is almost reduced to glaze, about 7 minutes. Season to taste with salt and pepper. Spoon sauce over fish; sprinkle with pine nuts and serve.

Cajun-Style Blackened Halibut

A nod to what could arguably be the dish of the eighties, blackened redfish. The technique works equally well with halibut.

4 SERVINGS

1 teaspoon salt
1 teaspoon minced fresh thyme
½ teaspoon dried oregano
½ teaspoon cayenne pepper
½ teaspoon sweet paprika
½ teaspoon ground black pepper
½ teaspoon fennel seeds, crushed
4 6-ounce halibut fillets
2 tablespoons olive oil

4 teaspoons butter

Preheat oven to 400°F. Mix first 7 ingredients in small bowl. Place fillets on baking sheet. Brush on both sides with 1 tablespoon oil. Sprinkle top of each with seasoning.

Heat heavy large skillet (preferably cast-iron) over high heat until very hot. Add remaining 1 tablespoon oil; swirl to coat. Place fillets, seasoned side down, in skillet. Cook until very brown on bottom, 1 minute. Return fillets, browned side up, to baking sheet. Place in oven; bake until just opaque in center, about 8 minutes. Top each with 1 teaspoon butter.

SEA BASS CRUSTED WITH PEPITAS AND CORIANDER

4 SERVINGS

2 tablespoons whole coriander seeds
1⅓ cups fresh breadcrumbs made
    from crustless sourdough bread
½ cup shelled pepitas, toasted
1 teaspoon salt

½ cup all purpose flour
2 large eggs
4 6-ounce sea bass fillets

4 tablespoons (½ stick) butter
2 tablespoons olive oil
    Lemon wedges

Heat heavy small skillet over medium heat. Add coriander; stir about 2 minutes. Transfer coriander to blender and blend until coarsely ground. Add breadcrumbs, pepitas and salt to blender; pulse until pepitas are coarsely chopped. Transfer mixture to baking sheet.

Place flour in pie dish. Whisk eggs to blend in medium bowl. Sprinkle fish with pepper. Dip both sides of each fish fillet into flour; shake off excess. Dip fish into eggs, then into breadcrumb mixture, coating completely.

Melt 2 tablespoons butter with 1 tablespoon oil in each of 2 heavy large skillets over medium-high heat. Add 2 fish fillets to each skillet and cook just until fish is opaque in center and coating is golden brown, about 3 minutes per side. Serve fish with lemon wedges.

PEPITAS, A.K.A. PUMPKIN SEEDS

Pepitas stand up well to cooking—they give a crunchy texture to all sorts of dishes, and their high oil content absorbs and complements adjacent flavors. Latin American markets carry pepitas in many forms: shelled, unshelled, toasted, raw, salted and not. But for most recipes, just buy the raw shelled ones, which are now available in most supermarkets.

SAUTÉED SHRIMP WITH LEMON-GARLIC BUTTER

The butter is also delicious over scallops. Serve the dish with steamed rice.

4 SERVINGS

½ cup dry white wine
2 tablespoons white wine vinegar
8 garlic cloves, minced
½ cup (1 stick) chilled butter,
    cut into ½-inch pieces
2 tablespoons fresh lemon juice

2 tablespoons olive oil
1½ pounds uncooked large shrimp,
    peeled, deveined
2 tablespoons grated lemon peel
1 tablespoon chopped fresh chives

Boil wine, vinegar and garlic in small saucepan until mixture is reduced to ¼ cup, about 4 minutes. Reduce heat to low. Whisk in butter, 1 piece at a time, allowing butter to melt before adding more. Remove from heat. Stir in lemon juice. Season with salt and pepper. Cover and keep warm.

Heat oil in large nonstick skillet over high heat. Sprinkle shrimp with salt and pepper. Add to skillet and sauté until shrimp are opaque in center, about 3 minutes. Transfer shrimp to plates. Drizzle lemon-garlic butter over. Sprinkle with lemon peel and chives and serve.

LEMON AID

Supermarkets offer a constant, reasonably priced supply of lemons, usually piled high and threatening to tumble at the slightest provocation. It's worth risking a landslide, though, in search of lemons that feel hefty for their size—a sign of juiciness. That's an important quality to look for because most lemony recipes get their zing from the juice. Others draw flavor from the zest (the bright yellow outermost layer of peel), but it's quite rare to find a recipe that calls for cooking entire lemon wedges or slices.

To extract the most juice, use the palm of your hand to press down firmly on a whole lemon, and roll it back and forth on the kitchen counter to rupture the membranes of the tiny sacs inside. Slice the lemon in half crosswise, and insert a fork into one of the halves. Then twist the fork while squeezing the lemon over a bowl to catch the juice. Since juice flows more freely at warmer temperatures, avoid refrigerating any lemons that will be squeezed. Expect 2½ to 3 tablespoons of juice from the average lemon.

The zest contains flavorful essential oils that can add a strong lemony taste to sweet or savory dishes. Whether you remove it with a vegetable peeler or a paring knife, a citrus zester or a grater, avoid the bitter white pith underneath. The average lemon offers up about 1 tablespoon of zest.

Mussels with Pernod and Cream

Start with a romaine salad tossed with Dijon vinaigrette, and pass rolls for dipping into the mussel broth. Lemon tarts from the bakery would be a nice finale.

2 SERVINGS; CAN BE DOUBLED

1⅓ cups sliced leeks (white and pale green parts only)
1¼ cups dry white wine
¼ cup diced red bell pepper
2 pounds mussels, scrubbed, debearded
½ cup whipping cream
3 tablespoons Pernod or other anise liqueur
3 tablespoons chopped fresh parsley

Combine sliced leeks, dry white wine and red bell pepper in large pot. Add mussels. Bring to boil over high heat. Cover pot and cook until mussels open, about 5 minutes. Using tongs, transfer mussels to medium bowl (discard any mussels that do not open). Add whipping cream and Pernod to pot; boil until liquid is slightly reduced, about 4 minutes. Mix in chopped parsley. Return mussels and any accumulated juices to pot. Simmer until mussels are warmed through, about 1 minute; season with salt and pepper. Serve mussels with broth.

SHELLING OUT MUSSELS

When eating mussels, Provençal natives forgo cutlery. Instead, they fish an empty shell from the bowl, then use it first as a spoon to scoop up the broth, then as tongs to pry the mussels out of their shells.

Brazilian Seafood Stew

The coconut milk can be found in the Asian foods section of most supermarkets.

6 TO 8 SERVINGS

4 tablespoons olive oil
2 tablespoons fresh lime juice
1½ pounds white fish fillets (such as red snapper or orange roughy), cut into 1-inch pieces
1½ cups chopped onion
1½ cups chopped green bell peppers
2 garlic cloves, chopped
¾ teaspoon dried crushed red pepper
2 cups chopped tomatoes
¾ cup canned unsweetened coconut milk
½ cup chopped fresh cilantro
½ cup chopped green onions
1¼ pounds uncooked medium shrimp, peeled, deveined

Whisk 2 tablespoons oil and lime juice in large bowl. Add fish and sprinkle generously with salt and pepper; stir to coat. Let stand 15 minutes.

Heat remaining 2 tablespoons oil in large pot over medium heat. Add onion, bell peppers, garlic and crushed red pepper; sauté 5 minutes. Mix in tomatoes, coconut milk, half of cilantro and half of green onions. Add shrimp and fish with marinade. Simmer until shrimp and fish are just opaque in center, about 5 minutes. Season stew with salt and pepper. Transfer to bowl. Sprinkle with remaining cilantro and green onions.

Poultry

SPICY CHICKEN CACCIATORE

4 SERVINGS

4 chicken breast halves with skin and bones
2 tablespoons olive oil
1 large red bell pepper, diced
4 garlic cloves, chopped
1 teaspoon fennel seeds
1 teaspoon dried oregano
½ teaspoon dried crushed red pepper
1 28-ounce can diced tomatoes in juice
¼ cup tomato paste

¼ cup dry red wine
1 tablespoon balsamic vinegar

1 pound spaghetti, freshly cooked

Sprinkle chicken with salt and pepper. Heat oil in large skillet over medium-high heat. Add chicken, skin side down, and sauté until brown, about 5 minutes. Turn chicken over; sauté 3 minutes. Transfer chicken to plate. Add bell pepper and next 4 ingredients to skillet; stir 2 minutes. Mix in tomatoes with juices, tomato paste, wine and vinegar. Return chicken to skillet; spoon some sauce over. Bring to boil. Cover, reduce heat to medium-low and simmer until chicken is cooked through, about 4 minutes per side.

Arrange spaghetti on large platter; top with chicken and sauce.

CHICKEN WITH HERBED VEGETABLE SAUCE

4 SERVINGS

4 skinless boneless chicken breast halves
2 tablespoons chopped fresh thyme
2 tablespoons olive oil
2 small zucchini, cut into thin strips
1 small leek (white and pale green parts only), cut into thin strips
4 2-inch-long pieces celery, cut into thin strips
½ medium carrot, cut into thin strips
3 garlic cloves, minced
12 ounces cherry tomatoes, halved
1 cup canned low-salt chicken broth
8 large fresh basil leaves, sliced

Sprinkle chicken with salt, pepper and half of thyme. Heat oil in heavy large skillet over medium-high heat. Add chicken; sauté 3 minutes per side. Transfer to plate. Add zucchini, leek, celery, carrot, garlic and remaining thyme.

Sauté until vegetables are crisp-tender, about 5 minutes. Add tomatoes. Return chicken to skillet, nestling chicken among vegetables. Pour in broth; bring to boil. Cover, reduce heat to medium-low and simmer until chicken is cooked through, about 5 minutes. Transfer chicken to platter. Add basil and boil until sauce thickens slightly, about 5 minutes. Season with salt and pepper; spoon sauce over chicken.

DEGLAZING DEBRIEFING

Deglazing is a technique that's often used when making gravies or sauces based on pan drippings. Simply remove whatever was cooked in the pan (meat, poultry, fish or vegetables), add a bit of liquid (broth or wine, usually) to the pan, then put the pan over heat to warm up the liquid and help loosen the browned bits. Using a wooden spoon or spatula, scrape up the bits while the heat reduces the liquid. The result is richly flavored sauce or gravy.

CORNMEAL-CRUSTED CHICKEN BREASTS

Here's a delightful variation on the fried-chicken theme, with cornmeal adding welcome crunch.

6 SERVINGS

1 cup fresh breadcrumbs made
　from crustless French bread
1 cup yellow cornmeal
2 tablespoons minced fresh parsley
2 tablespoons minced fresh thyme
1 teaspoon salt
½ teaspoon ground black pepper
½ cup Dijon mustard
2 large eggs
6 skinless boneless chicken breast
　halves

4 tablespoons (½ stick) butter
4 tablespoons olive oil

Lemon wedges

Preheat oven to 350°F. Mix 1 cup breadcrumbs, 1 cup yellow cornmeal, 2 tablespoons minced parsley, 2 tablespoons minced thyme, 1 teaspoon salt and ½ teaspoon pepper in large bowl. Whisk ½ cup Dijon mustard and 2 eggs in medium bowl to blend.

Using mallet or rolling pin, pound each chicken breast half between sheets of plastic wrap to ½- to ⅓-inch thickness. Dip pounded chicken first into mustard mixture and coat well, then into breadcrumb mixture and coat well; shake off excess breadcrumbs.

Melt 2 tablespoons butter with 2 tablespoons oil in heavy large skillet over medium-high heat. Add half of chicken to skillet; cook until golden, about 2 minutes per side. Transfer chicken to 13x9x2-inch glass baking dish. Repeat with remaining butter, oil and chicken.

Bake chicken until cooked through, about 8 minutes. Garnish with lemon wedges and serve.

ORANGE AND GINGER CHICKEN

4 SERVINGS

4 boneless chicken breast halves
   with skin
   All purpose flour
2 tablespoons (¼ stick) butter
1 tablespoon olive oil
4 teaspoons minced peeled fresh
   ginger
2 tablespoons brown sugar
1 teaspoon dry mustard
2 cups orange juice
2 teaspoons grated orange peel
¾ cup thinly sliced green onions

Sprinkle chicken with salt and pepper; dust with flour. Melt butter with oil in large skillet over medium-high heat. Add chicken; sauté until brown, about 3 minutes per side. Transfer chicken to plate. Add ginger to skillet; stir 1 minute. Add brown sugar and mustard and stir to blend into drippings. Add orange juice and orange peel. Simmer until sauce is slightly reduced, stirring occasionally, about 8 minutes. Return chicken and any accumulated juices to skillet. Simmer 3 minutes. Turn chicken over and add green onions. Simmer until chicken is cooked through and sauce is thick enough to coat spoon, about 3 minutes longer. Season sauce with salt and pepper. Transfer chicken and sauce to platter.

THE SKINNY ON CHICKEN SKIN

Contrary to popular belief, the fat in chicken skin does not transfer to the meat during cooking. This is particularly good news if you want to prepare such dishes as a whole roast chicken. The skin forms a protective layer, which seals in the moisture to prevent the chicken from drying out while it's in the oven. The resulting chicken meat turns out juicier, and you don't get that dry, hardened layer that forms when the meat is directly exposed to the heat. Leaving the skin on will also add flavor to the cooked meat.

Just to give you an idea of how much fat you can cut out by removing the skin before eating, a 3½-ounce serving of roasted chicken breast with the skin has about 193 calories and 7.6 grams of fat. The same size chicken breast without the skin has about 142 calories and only 3 grams of fat.

Another tip for reducing fat intake: Stick to the white meat (breast meat). A 3½-ounce portion of roasted dark meat (thigh and drumstick) with the skin contains about 232 calories and a whopping 13 grams of fat. The same amount of meat without the skin has about 159 calories and 7 grams of fat.

CHICKEN WITH MUSTARD CREAM ON WATERCRESS

For a side dish, serve couscous mixed with sautéed red bell pepper, carrots and dill. Buy a strawberry tart to finish.

2 SERVINGS; CAN BE DOUBLED

1 bunch watercress, stems trimmed
2 skinless boneless chicken breast halves

1 tablespoon butter
⅓ cup canned low-salt chicken broth
¼ cup whipping cream
2½ tablespoons honey Dijon mustard

Divide watercress between 2 plates. Place chicken between sheets of waxed paper. Using rolling pin, pound chicken to even ½-inch thickness. Peel off paper. Sprinkle chicken with salt and pepper.

Melt butter in heavy medium skillet over medium heat. Add chicken; sauté until cooked through, about 4 minutes per side. Place chicken atop watercress. Add broth, cream and mustard to skillet.

Boil until sauce thickens, whisking often, about 2 minutes. Season with salt and pepper. Spoon sauce over chicken.

SPICY GRILLED CHICKEN AND GREEN ONIONS
(COVER RECIPE)

Buy some carrot and celery sticks to dip into blue cheese dressing for a cool starter. Deli potato salad is good with the chicken, and classic Southern ambrosia—sliced oranges with coconut—is a refreshing end.

2 SERVINGS; CAN BE DOUBLED

2 tablespoons vegetable oil
1 tablespoon hot pepper sauce
2 teaspoons honey
1 teaspoon paprika
7 green onions
2 skinless boneless chicken breast halves

Prepare barbecue (medium-high heat). Whisk oil, hot sauce, honey and paprika in 9-inch glass pie dish to blend. Mince

1 green onion; mix into marinade. Transfer 2 tablespoons marinade to small bowl and reserve. Add chicken to marinade in pie dish and turn to coat. Let stand 10 minutes, turning occasionally.

Sprinkle chicken and remaining whole green onions with salt. Grill chicken and whole onions until chicken is cooked through and onions soften, turning occasionally, about 10 minutes. Transfer chicken and onions to plates. Drizzle with reserved 2 tablespoons marinade.

TURKEY TENDERLOINS WITH PESTO AND PROVOLONE CHEESE

Rice pilaf and roasted vegetables are good choices for side dishes. Using purchased pesto makes this dish a snap to prepare.

6 SERVINGS

4 turkey tenderloins (about 2¼ pounds)

8 tablespoons purchased pesto

3 ounces thinly sliced provolone cheese, cut into ½-inch-wide strips

Fresh basil sprigs (optional)

Preheat oven to 375°F. Cut each tenderloin lengthwise almost in half. Sprinkle inside and out with salt and pepper. Spread 1 tablespoon pesto inside each. Then insert cheese strips, dividing equally. Using toothpicks, skewer tenderloins closed. Brush each all over with 1 tablespoon pesto. Arrange tenderloins on rimmed baking sheet.

Bake tenderloins until thermometer inserted near center registers 160°F, about 20 minutes. Slice tenderloins crosswise into ¾-inch-thick rounds; arrange on serving platter. Whisk any juices and browned bits on baking sheet to blend; spoon over turkey. Garnish with basil sprigs, if desired, and serve.

TROPICAL PUNCH

Allen Susser, of Chef Allen's in Miami, blends bright fruit flavors into delicious sauces and marinades. Mango ketchup, tamarind-chili spicy grill sauce and papaya-pineapple barbecue sauce are three of the choices. Call 305-932-1101.

Meat

RIB-EYE STEAKS WITH BÉARNAISE BUTTER

Butter melting over a pan-fried steak mingles with its rosy juices, creating a luscious sauce right on the plate. For smaller appetites, these large steaks can be cut in half to serve four.

2 SERVINGS

¼ cup dry white wine

1 tablespoon minced shallot

¼ teaspoon dried tarragon

5 tablespoons butter, room temperature

1 tablespoon minced fresh tarragon

Olive oil

2 12-ounce rib-eye steaks (each about 1 to 1¼ inches thick)

Boil wine, shallot and dried tarragon in small saucepan until liquid evaporates, about 2 minutes. Cool completely.

Mix butter and fresh tarragon into shallot mixture. Season with salt and pepper. Form butter mixture into log; wrap in plastic and chill until firm. (*Can be made 3 days ahead. Keep chilled.*) Cut butter into ⅓-inch-thick slices. Bring to room temperature before continuing.

Brush large nonstick skillet with oil; heat over medium-high heat. Sprinkle steaks with salt and pepper; add to skillet. Cook to desired doneness, about 5 minutes per side for medium-rare. Overlap butter slices atop steaks and serve.

Beef Tenderloin with Garlic and Brandy

4 SERVINGS

4 6- to 7-ounce beef tenderloin
   steaks (each about 1 inch thick)
1 tablespoon olive oil
3 tablespoons chopped fresh parsley
3 large garlic cloves, chopped
⅔ cup canned beef broth
2 tablespoons brandy

Sprinkle steaks with salt and pepper. Heat oil in large skillet over medium-high heat. Add steaks; cook to desired doneness, about 5 minutes per side for medium-rare. Transfer steaks to platter. Add 2 tablespoons parsley and garlic to skillet; stir 30 seconds. Add broth, then brandy. Boil until juices are reduced to glaze, about 6 minutes. Spoon glaze over steaks. Sprinkle with remaining 1 tablespoon parsley.

The Searing Myth

Searing exposes meat to a very high temperature to brown it on the surface.

It was once thought that searing formed a waterproof crust through which the meat's juices and flavor could not escape. But, according to food scientist Harold McGee in *On Food and Cooking*, that is not true. Even so, there is one excellent reason to sear: flavor. While the brown crust that is formed by searing may not be waterproof, it *is* delicious.

Sirloin Patties with Vegetable Sauce
Pair this dish with rice pilaf or noodles.

4 SERVINGS

1 pound ground beef sirloin
1¼ cups canned chicken broth
⅓ cup finely crushed crackers
   (such as Ritz)
4 tablespoons minced fresh parsley
3 large garlic cloves, minced
¾ teaspoon salt
½ teaspoon ground black pepper
2 tablespoons olive oil

1 8-ounce potato, peeled, cut into
   ½-inch pieces
1 cup ½-inch pieces peeled carrots
1 cup ½-inch pieces celery
1 cup tomato sauce
¼ cup chopped pitted brine-cured
   green olives

Mix beef, ¼ cup broth, crackers, 2 tablespoons parsley, garlic, salt and pepper in large bowl. Shape mixture into 2½-inch-diameter, ½-inch-thick patties. Heat oil in heavy large skillet over medium heat. Working in 2 batches, sauté patties until brown and cooked through, about 5 minutes per side. Transfer to plate.

Add potato, carrots and celery to same skillet; sauté 5 minutes, scraping up browned bits. Add tomato sauce, olives and remaining 1 cup broth and 2 tablespoons parsley. Cover and simmer until vegetables are tender, about 15 minutes. Place patties in skillet atop vegetable sauce. Cover and simmer until heated through, about 10 minutes.

BEEF MEDALLIONS WITH COGNAC SAUCE

Serve Cabernet Sauvignon with the steaks.

2 SERVINGS

2 tablespoons (¼ stick) unsalted butter
¼ cup chopped shallots
1 teaspoon (packed) brown sugar
1 cup canned low-salt chicken broth
½ cup canned beef broth
½ cup Cognac or brandy
¼ cup whipping cream

2 4- to 5-ounce beef tenderloin steaks (each about 1 inch thick)

Fresh chives

Melt 1 tablespoon butter in heavy medium saucepan over medium heat. Add shallots and sauté until tender, about 4 minutes. Add brown sugar; stir 1 minute. Add chicken broth, beef broth and Cognac. Simmer until sauce is reduced to ½ cup, about 20 minutes. Add cream. (*Can be made 1 day ahead. Cover; chill.*)

Sprinkle steaks with salt and pepper. Melt 1 tablespoon butter in heavy medium skillet over medium-high heat. Add steaks; cook to desired doneness, about 4 minutes per side for rare. Transfer steaks to plates. Add sauce to skillet; bring to boil, scraping up any browned bits. Season to taste with salt and pepper.

Slice steaks; fan slices on plates. Top with sauce and garnish with chives.

A.1 ADVICE

Bottles of A.1 sauce have been a staple at summer barbecues for a long time. Now the folks who make it have hooked up with other grilling pros to spread cooking secrets discovered in the fires of experience. Call 888-217-8325, or point your mouse to www.a1steaksauce.com and you'll find tips and recipes from some of the country's top steak-house chefs. Those recipes, however do *not* include the formula for this 137-year-old secret sauce.

Veal Cutlets with Mushrooms and Tomatoes

4 SERVINGS

4 tablespoons olive oil
2 large garlic cloves, chopped
¾ teaspoon chopped fresh rosemary
12 ounces mushrooms, sliced
12 ounces plum tomatoes, seeded, chopped

1 pound thin veal cutlets
All purpose flour

1 cup canned low-salt chicken broth
½ cup dry white wine

Heat 2 tablespoons oil in heavy large saucepan over medium-high heat. Add garlic and rosemary; stir 30 seconds. Add mushrooms. Cover pan and cook 5 minutes, stirring occasionally. Uncover and sauté until mushrooms are golden brown, about 5 minutes longer. Add tomatoes and cook until softened, about 5 minutes. Set aside.

Sprinkle veal with salt and pepper. Dust with flour. Heat 1 tablespoon oil in heavy large skillet over medium-high heat. Add half of veal. Sauté until brown and cooked through, about 2 minutes per side. Transfer veal to platter; tent with foil to keep warm. Repeat with remaining 1 tablespoon oil and veal.

Add broth and wine to same skillet. Boil until reduced by half, scraping up browned bits, about 4 minutes. Add mushroom mixture and stir to blend. Season sauce to taste with salt and pepper; spoon over veal and serve.

SAUCY CHEF

Larry Forgione of New York's An American Place has fulfilled the American barbecue dream with his mango grilling sauce. It adds a sweet and tangy zing to meats, fish and vegetables. Call 888-735-6700 to order.

Veal Chops with Arugula Salad

An elegant and simple main course.

4 SERVINGS

6 tablespoons olive oil (preferably extra-virgin)
1 tablespoon balsamic vinegar

4 6- to 8-ounce veal loin chops (each about ¾ inch thick)
4 teaspoons ground sage

4 cups (packed) arugula leaves (about 4 large bunches)
⅓ cup chopped red onion

Whisk 3 tablespoons oil and vinegar in large bowl. Season to taste with salt and pepper; set dressing aside.

Place chops between 2 large pieces of plastic wrap on work surface, spacing apart. Using meat mallet, pound veal surrounding bone to ½-inch thickness. Rub each side of each chop with ½ teaspoon sage. Sprinkle with salt and pepper.

Heat remaining 3 tablespoons oil in heavy large skillet over medium-high heat. Add chops; cook about 3 minutes per side for medium-rare. Transfer to platter; cover and keep warm.

Whisk any drippings from skillet into dressing. Add arugula and red onion to dressing and toss to coat. Top chops with arugula salad and serve.

THE ARUGULA OF ITALY

Arugula is one of the fastest-growing vegetables around. You can plant it anytime and start picking it three weeks later. At that point, when it is tender and young, arugula is perhaps the single best salad green.

And arugula continues to grow almost regardless of the weather. As the leaves get bigger and the stems grow thicker, the flavor becomes peppery hot. This doesn't mean that it isn't worth eating —just strip the leaves off the stems and enjoy the fiery taste. Mature arugula makes excellent pesto (great on gnocchi); when chopped, it's a nice addition to potato or bean salads. It can also replace lettuce in sandwiches—an American innovation that is making its way back to the Old World.

Arugula is native to the Mediterranean, and the ancient Romans were quite fond of its sharpness. It grows wild everywhere—on the poorest, driest, most sun-drenched hillsides and in the rich soil of the fertile plains.

The wild green is called *ruchetta*, and the cultivated type is known as *rucola*. Both names have their roots in the Italian language and translate roughly as "garden rocket." Cultivated arugula has leaves that are flatter and broader than those of the wild kind. Almost all of the arugula we come across here—in supermarkets and in gardens—is the cultivated variety, but gardeners on both East and West coasts are growing plants from wild seeds.

For those without gardens, arugula can be found in bunches at farmers' markets, and it's becoming more readily available in grocery stores. Sometimes it's in the herb section, packed in little plastic cartons; other times you'll find it loose in the produce bins, or it might be sold prewashed in plastic bags. Unfortunately, just as supermarkets sell dandelion greens that are way too mature to eat, they also tend to offer old, tough arugula.

Lamb Chops with Asian Pear and Kiwi Salsa

Honey and mint are the special ingredients in this lovely lamb dish.

4 SERVINGS

2 small Asian pears, cored, diced
3 large kiwis, peeled, diced
6 tablespoons dried cranberries
¼ cup chopped green onions
2 tablespoons fresh lemon juice
3 tablespoons honey
3 tablespoons chopped fresh mint

8 1-inch-thick lamb rib chops

Combine pears, kiwis, cranberries, onions and lemon juice in medium bowl; mix in 2 tablespoons honey and 2 tablespoons chopped mint. Season salsa to taste with salt and pepper. Let stand 20 minutes, tossing occasionally.

Meanwhile, preheat broiler. Brush chops lightly on both sides with remaining 1 tablespoon honey; sprinkle with salt, pepper and remaining 1 tablespoon chopped fresh mint. Broil chops until cooked to desired doneness, about 5 minutes per side for medium-rare.

Transfer 2 lamb chops to each plate. Spoon salsa alongside and serve.

Pork Cutlets with Figs and Balsamic Vinegar

In this entrée, balsamic vinegar gives tartness to a cream sauce that balances nicely with the pork and figs. Sautéed spinach or chard would go well with the dish.

4 SERVINGS

8 ⅓-inch-thick slices center-cut pork loin
1½ tablespoons olive oil

1 tablespoon butter
¼ cup minced shallots
3 tablespoons balsamic vinegar
1 cup canned low-salt chicken broth
6 fresh ripe figs, quartered
½ cup whipping cream
1 tablespoon minced parsley

Preheat oven to 200°F. Sprinkle pork with salt and pepper. Heat 1 tablespoon oil in heavy large skillet over medium-high heat. Add 4 pork slices and sauté until brown, about 2 minutes per side. Transfer pork to baking sheet. Add remaining ½ tablespoon oil to skillet. Repeat with remaining 4 pork slices. Transfer pork to oven to keep warm.

Melt 1 tablespoon butter in same skillet over medium-high heat. Add shallots and sauté until tender, about 2 minutes. Add 2 tablespoons vinegar. Simmer until vinegar evaporates, scraping up any browned bits on bottom of skillet, about 1 minute. Add chicken broth. Simmer until mixture is reduced by half, about 4 minutes. Add figs and whipping cream. Simmer until sauce thickens slightly, about 4 minutes. Add remaining 1 tablespoon vinegar and any accumulated juices from pork. Simmer until sauce thickens enough to coat spoon, about 2 minutes longer. Season sauce to taste with salt and pepper.

Arrange pork on plates. Spoon sauce over. Sprinkle with parsley and serve.

RACK OF LAMB WITH SPICE-AND-PEPPER CRUST

Accompany this well-seasoned main course with a creamy potato gratin and purchased caponata drizzled with fresh lemon juice; serve apple pie for dessert.

2 SERVINGS; CAN BE DOUBLED

1 1¼- to 1½-pound rack of lamb, trimmed
1 teaspoon cumin seeds
1 teaspoon coriander seeds
1 teaspoon green peppercorns
2 large garlic cloves, chopped
1 tablespoon grated orange peel
1 tablespoon extra-virgin olive oil

Preheat oven to 450°F. Sprinkle lamb with salt and pepper. Enclose cumin, coriander and peppercorns in small resealable plastic bag. Using mallet, coarsely crush seeds and peppercorns. Add garlic, orange peel and oil to bag and mash to coarse paste. Smear paste over meat portion of lamb.

Place lamb, paste side up, in small baking pan. Roast lamb 10 minutes. Reduce heat to 400°F. Continue to roast until thermometer inserted into lamb registers 135°F for medium-rare, about 15 minutes longer. Cut lamb between bones into chops and serve.

ON THE LAMB

For an elegant entrée, try a tender and delicious rack of New Zealand lamb from Pilot Brands. Call 800-621-5262.

Vegetarian & Dairy

GRUYÈRE FONDUE WITH SALSA VERDE

Not a Mexican salsa, this Italian "green sauce" is made of fresh basil, parsley, garlic and a big splash of vermouth. Swirled atop the cheese mixture, the salsa verde adds a lovely marbled effect to the fondue.

4 TO 6 SERVINGS

⅓ cup (packed) fresh basil leaves
¼ cup chopped fresh parsley
¼ cup dry vermouth
1 tablespoon Dijon mustard
1 garlic clove
1½ pounds Gruyère cheese, shredded (about 5½ cups)
2 tablespoons cornstarch
1½ cups dry white wine

Bite-size pieces of focaccia or French bread, fresh fennel, steamed broccoli and cauliflower florets, cherry tomatoes and peeled cooked shrimp

Purée first 5 ingredients in blender until smooth. Transfer salsa verde to small bowl. Season to taste with salt and pepper. Cover tightly and let stand at room temperature. *(Can be prepared 2 hours ahead. Keep at room temperature.)*

Toss Gruyère with cornstarch in large bowl. Bring wine to simmer in heavy medium saucepan over medium heat. Add cheese to wine in 3 batches, whisking after each addition until cheese melts before adding more. Continue stirring until mixture is smooth and just begins to simmer (do not boil). Stir in half of salsa verde. Season with salt and pepper.

Transfer fondue to fondue pot. Spoon remaining salsa verde atop fondue. Swirl knife through fondue and salsa verde, creating marbled design. Set pot over candle or canned heat burner. Serve with focaccia, vegetables and shrimp.

FACTS ON FONDUE

Fondue is French for "melted." The dish is of Swiss origin, and it is most often made with the Swiss cheeses Emmenthal and/or Gruyère. Other ingredients include a little cornstarch or flour for texture, some alcohol (kirsch, white wine, hard cider or beer), some garlic and lemon juice. Kirsch is also frequently served alongside, and is said to aid in digestion of this heavy, dairy-rich dish.

The cheese is melted and presented in a fondue pot, which sits atop a metal stand and has a built-in gas heat source below. Fondue must be served over heat so that the smooth, creamy texture of the cheese is maintained. Cubes of bread are the classic accompaniment. They are speared with long, three-pronged forks specially made for the task, then swirled in the cheese a few times before eating.

Superstitions abound: Never drink a cold beverage with fondue, as it will cause terrible indigestion. And try not to drop your cube of bread into the cheese. If that happens, you will owe the host a bottle of wine.

When the cheese is almost gone, turn down the heat a bit and let the layer on the bottom of the fondue pot form a crust called the *religieuse*. Traditionally, this delicacy is divided among the guests.

Pasta & Risotto

PASTA WITH TOMATOES, ZUCCHINI AND PESTO

This delicious pasta uses store-bought pesto.

6 SERVINGS

¼ cup olive oil
4 cups ½-inch cubes zucchini (about 22 ounces)
1½ cups chopped onion
2 large garlic cloves, chopped
1 28-ounce can diced tomatoes in juice

1 pound spaghetti

1 7-ounce package purchased pesto
½ cup thinly sliced fresh basil
Grated Parmesan cheese

Heat oil in heavy large pot over medium-high heat. Add zucchini, onion and garlic and sauté until zucchini is crisp-tender, about 5 minutes. Add tomatoes with juices and simmer until almost all liquid evaporates, about 8 minutes.

Meanwhile, cook pasta in large pot of boiling salted water until just tender but still firm to bite. Drain; return to pot.

Add pesto to pasta and toss to coat. Add zucchini mixture and toss over low heat to combine. Mix in basil. Season pasta with salt and pepper. Transfer pasta to large bowl. Serve, passing Parmesan cheese separately.

Pasta with Greens, Goat Cheese and Raisins

It used to be that beets were sent to the market without the greens, which had been discarded. Now both are sold, often separately. Your best bet is to buy beets that have the greens intact; that way, you can partner this unique sweet and savory pasta with the perfect side dish: roasted fresh beets.

4 TO 6 SERVINGS

⅓ cup golden raisins
⅓ cup fresh lemon juice

4 tablespoons olive oil
1½ cups finely chopped red onion
3 garlic cloves, minced
1 bunch red or green Swiss chard
  (about 12 ounces), stems
  trimmed, leaves coarsely chopped
1 bunch beet greens (about 6
  ounces), stems trimmed, leaves
  coarsely chopped

2 tablespoons minced peeled
  fresh ginger
1½ tablespoons grated lemon peel

1 pound orecchiette (little
  ear-shaped pasta)
5 ounces soft fresh goat cheese
  (such as Montrachet)

Combine raisins and lemon juice in small bowl. Set aside.

Heat 2 tablespoons oil in heavy large pot over medium-low heat. Add onion and sauté until tender, about 8 minutes. Add garlic and sauté until fragrant, about 1 minute. Add Swiss chard, beet greens and raisin mixture. Cover and cook until greens wilt, about 5 minutes. Mix in ginger and lemon peel. Season greens to taste with salt and pepper.

Meanwhile, cook pasta in large pot of boiling salted water until tender but still firm to bite. Drain. Return pasta to pot. Toss pasta with remaining 2 table-spoons olive oil. Add greens and goat cheese. Toss to combine. Season to taste with salt and pepper. Transfer pasta to large bowl and serve.

Fusilli with Fresh Tomato and Olive Sauce

Since the tomatoes in the sauce are cooked just briefly, this dish is a breeze to make.

6 SERVINGS

¼ cup olive oil
1 cup Kalamata olives or other
  brine-cured black olives, pitted,
  chopped
1 medium onion, chopped
6 garlic cloves, chopped
½ teaspoon dried crushed red pepper
1½ pounds plum tomatoes
  (about 8 large), chopped
2 tablespoons tomato paste
2 tablespoons red wine vinegar
1 pound fusilli, freshly cooked

1½ cups coarsely grated Parmesan
  cheese (about 4 ounces)
1 cup chopped fresh basil

Heat olive oil in heavy large pot over
medium-high heat. Add olives, chopped
onion, chopped garlic and crushed red
pepper and sauté until onion begins to
soften, about 4 minutes. Add tomatoes
and tomato paste and stir until tomatoes
are just warmed through, about 2
minutes. Mix in red wine vinegar. Add
cooked pasta, 1 cup Parmesan cheese
and fresh basil and toss to combine.
Season to taste with salt and pepper.
Transfer to large bowl. Serve with
remaining Parmesan cheese.

Tuna and Vegetable Fettuccine with Lemon Breadcrumbs

*Both easy and inexpensive, tuna-noodle
casserole stretched proteins and carbohy-
drates to the limits and fed at least a gener-
ation of American kids very well. Canned
tuna will never go away, but fresh tuna has
joined it as a culinary staple, and it stars in
this deconstructed version of the classic. All
the elements that make tuna casserole so
appealing and comforting are here, just
slightly rearranged. And there's no need to
serve this on a cafeteria tray: It's good
enough for your best china.*

6 SERVINGS

7 tablespoons butter
1 tablespoon grated lemon peel
2 cups fresh breadcrumbs

2 cups whipping cream
8 ounces cherry tomatoes, halved
1 cup frozen petite peas, thawed
1 pound fresh tuna, cut into

½-inch pieces
1 pound fresh fettuccine
1 cup freshly grated Parmesan
  cheese
2 tablespoons fresh minced parsley

Melt 4 tablespoons butter in heavy medium skillet over medium heat. Add
lemon peel; sauté 1 minute. Add breadcrumbs; sauté until golden, about 5 minutes. Season with salt and pepper.

Combine cream, tomatoes, peas
and 3 tablespoons butter in large deep
skillet. Simmer over medium heat until
sauce begins to thicken, about 3 minutes. Add tuna and simmer until tuna is
cooked through, about 3 minutes.
Season to taste with salt and pepper.

Meanwhile, cook pasta in large pot
of boiling salted water until just tender.
Drain. Add pasta, cheese and parsley to
sauce; toss. Season with salt and pepper.

Divide pasta among plates. Sprinkle
with lemon breadcrumbs and serve.

NO MORE TEARS

Chopping onions (or garlic or shallots, for that matter—they all are part of the same family) releases a sulfuric compound. The chemical reacts with the saline in your eyes to create a mild sulfuric acid. Your eyes handle the attack by producing lots of tears to rinse the acid away.

The National Onion Association recommends refrigerating onions for an hour or so before cutting them to slow down the release of the irritating compound. Because the chemical is more concentrated in the base of the onion, don't cut the bottom (root end) off the onion before you start slicing. Cut off the top, and peel the skin from the sides of the onion. Cut a small slice off one side of the onion so that the onion can rest flat on the cutting surface. Slice until you get to the base, which you can then discard. If all else fails, you can wear protective goggles.

LINGUINE WITH SUN-DRIED TOMATO PESTO

Imported from Italy early in the decade, sun-dried tomatoes seduced the nation. Two other obsessions were pasta and pesto. All those ingredients combine here in a dish that doesn't age.

4 TO 6 SERVINGS

½ cup (packed) fresh basil leaves
¼ cup blanched slivered almonds, toasted
¼ cup drained oil-packed sun-dried tomatoes
1 garlic clove
⅛ teaspoon dried crushed red pepper
¼ cup extra-virgin olive oil
½ cup water
⅔ cup grated Parmesan cheese

1 pound linguine

Blend first 5 ingredients in processor until nuts are finely chopped. With machine running, gradually add oil, then ½ cup water, blending until almost smooth. Transfer pesto to bowl. Mix in ⅓ cup cheese. Season to taste with salt.

Cook linguine in large pot of boiling salted water until just tender but still firm to bite, stirring occasionally. Drain, reserving 1 cup cooking water. Return pasta to pot. Add pesto and toss to coat, adding enough reserved water to form thin sauce. Season with salt and pepper. Serve, passing remaining cheese.

PEANUT NOODLES WITH GINGERED VEGETABLES AND TOFU

Pretty and delicious, this pasta has plenty of vegetables, lots of snap and crunch, and a terrific Asian-style peanut sauce.

6 SERVINGS

2 tablespoons peanut oil
2 tablespoons minced fresh ginger
8 ounces broccoli, tops cut into florets, stems peeled, cut into thin strips
1 large carrot, peeled, cut into thin strips
1 celery stalk, thinly sliced
8 green onions, white parts cut into thin strips, green parts chopped
1 medium zucchini, cut lengthwise in half, then crosswise into ⅓-inch-thick slices
1 medium-size yellow crookneck squash, cut lengthwise in half, then crosswise into ⅓-inch-thick slices
1 red bell pepper, cut into thin strips
2 tablespoons dry Sherry
10 ounces extra-firm or firm tofu, cut into ½-inch pieces
12 ounces spaghetti, freshly cooked Chinese Peanut Sauce (see recipe)
1 cup lightly salted roasted peanuts

Heat peanut oil in large nonstick skillet over medium-high heat. Add ginger and stir 30 seconds. Add broccoli, carrot and celery and sauté 5 minutes. Add white parts of green onions, zucchini, yellow squash, bell pepper and Sherry and sauté until vegetables are crisp-tender, about 3 minutes longer. Add tofu and stir gently until heated through, about 2 minutes. Season to taste with salt and pepper.

Place spaghetti in large bowl. Add Chinese Peanut Sauce and toss to coat. Transfer to platter. Top with vegetable mixture. Sprinkle with peanuts and chopped green parts of green onions.

CHINESE PEANUT SAUCE

MAKES ABOUT 1¼ CUPS

½ cup creamy peanut butter (do not use old-fashioned or freshly ground)
2 tablespoons soy sauce
4 teaspoons minced garlic
½ cup hot water
¼ cup chopped fresh cilantro
3 tablespoons apple cider vinegar
2 teaspoons sugar
¾ teaspoon dried crushed red pepper

Mix peanut butter, soy sauce and garlic in medium bowl. Whisk in ½ cup hot water. Add remaining ingredients; whisk to blend. Season with salt and pepper. Let stand at room temperature 1 hour or cover and refrigerate up to 1 day.

Fettuccine Quatro Formaggi

Except for the Parmesan cheese, which is pretty much a requirement, this ultra-cheesy cousin of fettuccine Alfredo can be made with any number of four-cheese combinations.

8 SERVINGS

1 pound spinach fettuccine

1½ cups whipping cream
¾ cup crumbled Gorgonzola cheese
⅔ cup grated provolone cheese
½ cup crumbled soft fresh goat cheese (such as Montrachet)
¼ cup (½ stick) butter
½ teaspoon dried crushed red pepper
¼ teaspoon ground nutmeg

¾ cup freshly grated Parmesan cheese
¼ cup pine nuts, toasted

Cook pasta in pot of boiling salted water until just tender but still firm to bite.

Meanwhile, combine cream and next 6 ingredients in heavy large saucepan. Whisk over medium heat until mixture simmers and is smooth.

Drain pasta; return to same pot. Add cream sauce and Parmesan to pasta; toss to coat. Season with salt and pepper. Sprinkle with pine nuts and serve.

Penne with Sausage, Wild Mushrooms and Spinach

Button mushrooms would also be fine here.

4 SERVINGS

3 tablespoons olive oil
¾ pound fully cooked pork, chicken or turkey sausages, thickly sliced into rounds
¾ pound fresh wild mushrooms (such as crimini or stemmed shiitake), thickly sliced
¾ cup chopped shallots
5 garlic cloves, minced
½ teaspoon dried crushed red pepper
1 10-ounce package ready-to-use spinach leaves

1¼ cups canned low-salt chicken broth
¾ pound penne pasta, freshly cooked
2 cups (about 8 ounces) grated provolone or mozzarella cheese

Heat oil in heavy large pot over medium-high heat. Add sausages, mushrooms, shallots, garlic and crushed red pepper. Sauté until mushrooms begin to brown, about 10 minutes. Add spinach and broth; toss until spinach wilts, about 2 minutes. Add pasta and cheese; toss until cheese melts and sauce coats pasta, about 3 minutes. Season with salt and pepper.

Risotto with Peas and Green Onions

If you like, sauté some wild mushrooms and stir them into the finished risotto.

4 FIRST-COURSE OR
SIDE-DISH SERVINGS

3 tablespoons butter
¾ cup chopped green onions
½ teaspoon chopped fresh thyme
   or ¼ teaspoon dried
¾ cup arborio or medium-grain
   white rice
2½ cups (or more) canned low-salt
   chicken broth
¾ cup frozen petite peas, thawed
1 cup grated Parmesan cheese

Melt butter in heavy large saucepan over medium heat. Add green onions and thyme and sauté until onions wilt, about 1 minute. Add rice and stir to coat. Add 2½ cups broth and bring to boil. Reduce heat to medium-low and simmer 15 minutes, stirring occasionally. Mix in peas. Simmer until rice is tender and mixture is creamy, adding more broth by ¼ cupfuls if risotto is dry and stirring often, about 5 minutes. Mix in ⅓ cup cheese; season with salt and pepper. Serve risotto, passing remaining cheese separately.

Penne with Turkey and Wild Mushrooms

This spicy pasta dish is a real treat for mushroom lovers. Use as many different varieties as you can find.

4 TO 6 SERVINGS

1 pound penne

4 tablespoons olive oil
1 red bell pepper, chopped
1 tablespoon chopped fresh thyme
   or 1½ teaspoons dried
2 large garlic cloves, chopped
1 teaspoon dried crushed red pepper
1¼ pounds ground turkey
1 pound assorted fresh wild
   mushrooms (such as crimini;
   stemmed shiitake; portobello,
   dark gills scraped away), sliced
5 green onions, chopped
1⅓ cups canned low-salt chicken broth
2½ cups grated Parmesan cheese
½ cup dry white wine

Cook pasta in large pot of boiling salted water until tender but still firm to bite, stirring occasionally to prevent sticking. Drain very well. Set pasta aside.

Heat 2 tablespoons olive oil in heavy large pot over medium-high heat. Add bell pepper, thyme, garlic and crushed red pepper; sauté 2 minutes. Add ground turkey to pot. Sauté turkey until cooked through, breaking up turkey with back of fork, about 5 minutes. Using slotted spoon, transfer turkey mixture to large bowl.

Heat remaining 2 tablespoons oil in same pot over medium-high heat. Add mushrooms and green onions and sauté until mushrooms are tender and brown, about 6 minutes. Add turkey mixture, broth, 1½ cups Parmesan cheese, wine and pasta. Cook until sauce thickens enough to coat pasta, tossing often, about 3 minutes. Season to taste with salt and pepper. Serve, passing remaining Parmesan cheese separately.

QUICK SAUCE OR DIP

Whether nibbled on crackers or tossed with pasta, the tangy artichoke-lemon pesto from Bella Cucina Artful Food is perfect for easy summer entertaining. Call 800-580-5674.

PENNE WITH SHRIMP, ASPARAGUS AND SUN-DRIED TOMATOES

A quick and flavorful pasta dish that's special enough for company.

4 SERVINGS

½ cup drained oil-packed sun-dried
   tomatoes (about 2½ ounces),
   sliced, 2 tablespoons oil reserved
1 pound asparagus, trimmed, cut
   on diagonal into ½-inch pieces
1¼ pounds uncooked shrimp,
   peeled, deveined
½ cup chopped fresh basil
2 large garlic cloves, chopped
½ teaspoon dried oregano
¼ teaspoon dried crushed red pepper
1¾ cups canned low-salt chicken broth
½ cup dry white wine
2 tablespoons tomato paste

12 ounces penne pasta
¾ cup grated Parmesan cheese

Heat oil reserved from tomatoes in heavy large skillet over medium-high heat. Add asparagus and sauté until crisp-tender, about 5 minutes. Using slotted spoon, transfer asparagus to bowl. Add sun-dried tomatoes, shrimp, ¼ cup basil, garlic, oregano and crushed red pepper to same skillet and sauté until shrimp are just opaque in center, about 3 minutes. Transfer shrimp mixture to bowl with asparagus. Add broth, wine and tomato paste to same skillet. Boil until sauce thickens slightly, stirring occasionally, about 6 minutes.

Cook pasta in large pot of boiling salted water until tender but still firm to bite. Drain; return pasta to same pot. Add shrimp mixture, sauce, remaining ¼ cup basil and cheese to pasta. Toss over medium heat until warmed through and sauce coats pasta. Season with salt and pepper and serve.

Sandwiches, Wraps & Pizzas

THE BEST BLTS

Basil mayonnaise and avocado slices add an extra dimension to the good old bacon, lettuce and tomato sandwich. Bloody Marys would go nicely with them.

6 SERVINGS

2½ cups (lightly packed) fresh basil leaves
1 cup mayonnaise
¼ cup (½ stick) butter, room temperature

12 thick-sliced bacon strips (about 1 pound)

12 ½-inch-thick slices fresh country-style white bread
3 large tomatoes, cut into ¼-inch-thick rounds

2 ripe avocados, pitted, peeled, sliced
1 red onion, thinly sliced
6 lettuce leaves

Mix basil, mayonnaise and butter in processor until basil is finely chopped and mixture is well blended. Season to taste with salt and pepper. (*Can be made 1 day ahead. Cover and refrigerate.*)

Cook bacon in heavy large skillet over medium-high heat until crisp, about 8 minutes. Transfer to paper towels; drain.

Spread half of mayonnaise mixture over 1 side of 6 bread slices. Top each with 2 tomato slices. Sprinkle tomatoes with salt and pepper. Top tomato slices with avocado, then with bacon strips, onion and lettuce. Spread remaining mayonnaise mixture over remaining 6 bread slices. Place bread slices atop lettuce. Cut sandwiches in half and serve.

OFF-COLOR AVOCADOS

A good tip for combating the discoloration of a cut avocado is to squeeze some lemon juice over the exposed avocado flesh.

The avocado turns brown or black because of a chemical reaction called oxidation. When an avocado is sliced open, the inside of the fruit is exposed to oxygen, which changes the color of the avocado. The acid in lemon juice forms a seal on the surface of the avocado flesh that slows down the discoloration.

The California Avocado Commission suggests bathing the avocado in a mixture of water and a little vinegar; the acid in vinegar plays the same role as the acid in lemon juice. We've also found in our test kitchen that rinsing the cut surface of the avocado under cold running water can hold off oxidation for a few hours.

HAMBURGERS WITH MUSTARD AND MIXED HERBS

With the burgers, put out ketchup, mayonnaise, mustard and sliced pickles.

MAKES 8

2 pounds lean ground beef
½ cup finely chopped red onion
⅓ cup chopped fresh basil
¼ cup chopped fresh parsley
2 tablespoons chopped fresh thyme
2 tablespoons Worcestershire sauce
2 tablespoons Dijon mustard

8 ½- to ¾-inch-thick red onion slices
2 tablespoons olive oil
8 hamburger buns, split, toasted
8 lettuce leaves
8 tomato slices

Gently mix first 7 ingredients in medium bowl until just blended. Shape into eight ½- to ¾-inch-thick patties. (*Can be made 8 hours ahead. Cover and refrigerate.*)

Prepare barbecue (medium-high heat). Brush onion slices with oil. Sprinkle patties and onions with salt and pepper. Grill to desired doneness, about 5 minutes per side for medium; grill onions until tender, about 5 minutes per side. Place patties on bottom halves of buns. Top with grilled onions, lettuce, tomato and top halves of buns.

MUSTARD GREEN

Watercress mustard from Laurent du Clos adds garden-fresh flavor to sandwiches, dips and potato salads. Call Salumeria at 800-400-5916 to order.

Smoked-Turkey Tea Sandwiches with Arugula Mayonnaise

Try the arugula mayonnaise on burgers, and chicken and tuna sandwiches, too.

6 SERVINGS

½ cup mayonnaise
⅓ cup (packed) coarsely chopped arugula leaves plus 30 whole arugula leaves (about 4 large bunches total)
1 tablespoon minced shallot
1 tablespoon chopped fresh parsley
½ teaspoon grated lemon peel

12 thin slices firm white sandwich bread, crusts trimmed
10 ounces thinly sliced smoked turkey

Mix mayonnaise, chopped arugula, shallot, parsley and lemon peel in small bowl. Season with salt and pepper.

Place bread slices on work surface.

Spread mayonnaise mixture on each slice, dividing equally. Top 6 bread slices with turkey, dividing equally. Place 5 arugula leaves atop turkey on each. Top with remaining 6 bread slices, mayonnaise side down, pressing to adhere. Cut each sandwich diagonally into quarters.

Grilled Blue Cheese Sandwiches with Walnuts and Watercress

8 SERVINGS

1 cup crumbled blue cheese (about 8 ounces)
½ cup finely chopped toasted walnuts
16 slices whole wheat bread, trimmed into crustless 3-inch squares
16 small watercress sprigs

6 tablespoons (¾ stick) butter

Divide cheese and walnuts equally among 8 bread squares. Top each with 2 watercress sprigs. Sprinkle with pepper and top with remaining bread squares, making 8 sandwiches total. Press together gently to adhere. (*Can be made 4 hours ahead. Cover and chill.*)

Melt 3 tablespoons butter in large nonstick griddle or skillet over medium heat. Cook 4 sandwiches on griddle until golden brown and cheese melts, about 3 minutes per side. Transfer to cutting board. Repeat with remaining 3 tablespoons butter and 4 sandwiches.

Cut sandwiches diagonally in half. Transfer to plates and serve.

GOAT CHEESE AND WATERCRESS TEA SANDWICHES

The genteel ladies' tea, at which guests wore hats and white gloves and nibbled tiny sandwiches, was very much a part of home entertaining during the thirties. Borrowed from the British, it was a trend that flickered and then died out, but has now come back in homes and hotels across the country. These modern tea sandwiches are more savory than sweet, and would go well with a glass of Sherry if you're in need of something a little stronger than Earl Grey.

8 SERVINGS

2 5½-ounce logs soft fresh goat
   cheese (such as Montrachet),
   room temperature
½ cup chopped watercress leaves
16 thin slices cinnamon-raisin, date
   or whole wheat sandwich bread,
   crusts trimmed

5 tablespoons (about) unsalted
   butter, room temperature
¾ cup finely chopped toasted pecans
   Watercress sprigs (for garnish)

Mix cheese and chopped watercress in medium bowl. Season with salt. Spread mixture evenly over 8 bread slices. Top with remaining bread. Butter edges of sandwiches. Cut sandwiches diagonally in half.

Place pecans on plate. Dip buttered edges of sandwiches into pecans. Arrange sandwiches on platter. Garnish with watercress sprigs. (*Can be made 8 hours ahead. Cover sandwiches tightly; chill.*)

PEANUT BUTTER, BANANA AND DATE SANDWICHES

4 SERVINGS

2 whole wheat pita breads
8 tablespoons chunky or smooth
   old-fashioned peanut butter
6 pitted dates, chopped
8 teaspoons honey
2 ripe bananas, peeled, sliced

Lightly toast pita breads; cut each in half crosswise. Open pita pockets. Spread 2 tablespoons peanut butter on 1 side of the inside of each pita pocket. Sprinkle chopped dates over peanut butter, dividing equally. Drizzle honey over. Divide banana slices among pita pockets; close sandwiches, pressing slightly to adhere.

Spicy Turkey Sloppy Joes

Jean Anderson, author of The American Century Cookbook, *traces the origin of sloppy joes to the depression-era 1930s, and the popularity of this messy groundbeef sandwich increased markedly in the fifties and sixties. We update it with ground turkey, canned diced chilies and ale.*

6 SERVINGS

3 tablespoons olive oil
1½ pounds ground turkey
1 large green bell pepper, chopped
4 large garlic cloves, chopped
3 tablespoons chili powder
1¼ cups ale or beer
¾ cup bottled chili sauce or ketchup
1 4-ounce can diced green chilies
2 tablespoons Worcestershire sauce
1 cup finely chopped green onions

6 sourdough rolls, split, toasted
2 cups shredded romaine lettuce
    or packaged garden salad mix

Heat oil in heavy large pot over medium-high heat. Add turkey, green pepper and garlic and sauté until turkey is no longer pink, breaking up meat with back of fork, about 10 minutes. Mix in chili powder; stir 1 minute. Add next 4 ingredients. Reduce heat to medium-low and simmer until mixture thickens, stirring often, about 15 minutes. Mix in green onions; season with salt and pepper.

Arrange roll bottoms on plates. Spoon sloppy joe mixture over; top with lettuce and roll tops.

Black Bean and Vegetable Wraps

Any mixture of vegetables you have on hand would make a great filling. Serve the wraps with purchased salsa and sour cream.

4 SERVINGS

1½ tablespoons olive oil
2 large garlic cloves, minced
1 cup diced red bell pepper
1 cup diced yellow bell pepper
1 cup ½-inch pieces zucchini
1 cup ½-inch pieces peeled
    butternut squash
1 cup chopped red onion
2 teaspoons ground cumin
1 15-ounce can black beans, drained
1 cup (packed) grated hot pepper
    Monterey Jack cheese

4 9- to 10-inch-diameter flour
    tortillas (burrito size)
4 tablespoons chopped fresh
    cilantro

Heat olive oil in heavy large skillet over medium-high heat. Add garlic and stir 30 seconds. Add bell peppers, zucchini, squash and onion and sauté until crisptender, about 8 minutes. Mix in cumin and sauté until vegetables are tender, about 2 minutes longer. Season with salt and pepper. Place beans in large bowl; mash coarsely with fork.

Mix in vegetables and cheese.

Place tortillas on work surface. Spoon ¼ of filling down center of each. Sprinkle each with 1 tablespoon cilantro. Roll up tortillas, enclosing filling. Arrange wraps, seam side down, on baking sheet. *(Can be made 1 hour ahead. Let stand at room temperature.)*

Preheat oven to 350°F. Cover wraps with foil. Bake until filling is just heated through, about 10 minutes. Cut each wrap into 2 or 3 sections.

FLATBREAD PIZZAS WITH OLIVES, FETA AND ARTICHOKES

Deli cucumber salad and one of the new microwavable soups, such as savory lentil or spicy rice and bean, make great side dishes. End with purchased fresh fruit salad.

2 SERVINGS; CAN BE DOUBLED

2 6-inch-diameter whole wheat pita breads, cut horizontally in half, or one 24x9-inch soft Armenian lavash bread, halved crosswise

1 6.5-ounce jar marinated artichoke hearts, drained, marinade reserved, large pieces halved

1 5-ounce container sun-dried tomato- and basil-flavored feta cheese spread or 1½ cups crumbled flavored feta cheese

1 14.5-ounce can diced tomatoes with Italian herbs, drained well

1 cup pitted Kalamata olives or other brine-cured black olives, coarsely chopped

2 teaspoons dried oregano

Preheat oven to 450°F. Place breads on 2 baking sheets. Brush breads with some of artichoke marinade. Bake until just beginning to color, about 3 minutes. Cool on sheets 5 minutes.

Spread breads almost to edges with feta spread or sprinkle with crumbled feta cheese. Top with tomatoes, olives, oregano and artichokes. Drizzle with remaining artichoke marinade.

Bake pizzas until heated through, about 4 minutes. Cut into wedges.

SPICY BEEF AND SAUSAGE TACOS

Allow guests to fill their own taco shells with the spicy filling and assorted toppings. If you prefer soft tacos, use warm flour tortillas instead—or offer both versions.

MAKES 16

¼ cup olive oil

2 cups chopped red bell peppers

4 teaspoons minced garlic

1 pound ground beef

1 pound hot Italian sausages, casings removed

1 1¼-ounce package taco seasoning mix

½ cup chopped fresh cilantro
Hot pepper sauce

16 purchased corn taco shells

Grated cheddar cheese
Chopped red onion
Diced peeled avocado
Chopped tomatoes
Shredded lettuce

Heat oil in heavy large skillet over medium-high heat. Add bell peppers and garlic and sauté 1 minute. Add beef and sausage; sauté until brown, breaking up pieces with back of spoon, about 5 minutes. Sprinkle seasoning mix over; sauté 3 minutes longer. Add cilantro. Mix in enough pepper sauce to season to taste.

Transfer beef mixture to large bowl; place in center of platter. Surround with taco shells. Place cheese, onion, avocado, tomatoes and lettuce in bowls and serve.

DUCK SAUSAGE PIZZA WITH GREEN ONIONS AND TOMATO

Wolfgang Puck gets the credit for redefining pizza at his trend-setting Spago restaurant in West Hollywood. The inventive pizzas came topped with everything from goat cheese and Black Forest ham to artichokes and exotic mushrooms. Duck sausage pizzas, like this one, were a real hit.

4 SERVINGS

1 tablespoon extra-virgin olive oil
2 garlic cloves, minced
⅛ teaspoon dried crushed red pepper

1 10-ounce fully baked thin pizza crust (such as Boboli)
1½ cups (packed) grated mozzarella cheese (about 6 ounces)
½ cup chopped tomato
½ teaspoon dried oregano
2 smoked duck, chicken or turkey sausages, sliced
⅓ cup finely chopped green onions
½ cup freshly grated Parmesan cheese (about 1½ ounces)

Minced fresh parsley

Position rack in center of oven and preheat to 450°F. Mix olive oil, minced garlic and dried crushed red pepper in small bowl. Place pizza crust on rimless baking sheet. Sprinkle grated mozzarella cheese over all but 1-inch border of crust. Top mozzarella with chopped tomato, then oregano, sliced sausages, chopped green onions and grated Parmesan, in that order. Drizzle garlic-oil mixture over pizza.

Bake pizza until crust edges are crisp and brown and cheese melts, about 15 minutes. Sprinkle pizza with minced fresh parsley. Cut pizza into wedges and then serve immediately.

MEXICAN-STYLE CHICKEN SANDWICHES

4 SERVINGS

⅔ cup mayonnaise
2 tablespoons fresh lime juice
1½ teaspoons grated lime peel

1 15- to 16-ounce can black beans, drained, 2 tablespoons liquid reserved
1½ teaspoons ground cumin
4 French rolls, split horizontally, lightly toasted

4 skinless boneless chicken breast halves

¾ teaspoon cayenne pepper
1 tablespoon olive oil
4 ¼-inch-thick slices hot pepper Monterey Jack cheese

2 medium tomatoes, sliced
1 large avocado, peeled, pitted, sliced

Whisk mayonnaise, lime juice and lime peel in small bowl to blend; season with salt and pepper.

Stir beans and cumin in small skillet over medium heat until heated through, about 5 minutes. Add reserved bean liquid. Using fork, mash beans in skillet to coarse paste. Season to taste with salt and pepper. Arrange French roll bottoms on plates. Spread with bean mixture.

Sprinkle chicken with ¾ teaspoon cayenne pepper and salt. Heat 1 tablespoon olive oil in heavy large skillet over medium-high heat. Add chicken to skillet and sauté until just cooked through, about 4 minutes per side. Top chicken with cheese slices. Cover skillet, reduce heat to low and cook until cheese melts, about 1 minute.

Place chicken on bean mixture. Top with tomato, then avocado. Spread lime mayonnaise generously on cut side of each roll top; press onto sandwiches.

GREEN GIANTS

Howard's Choice extra-large avocados are wonderful in omelets and sandwiches, and their smooth, creamy flesh makes superb guacamole. Call 888-765-7667.

Breakfast & Brunch

SHIITAKE SCRAMBLED EGGS AND CAVIAR ON TOASTS

14 SERVINGS

6 tablespoons (¾ stick) butter
10 ounces shiitake mushrooms,
    stemmed, thinly sliced
1 teaspoon grated lemon peel

10 large eggs
¼ cup minced fresh chives
½ teaspoon salt
½ teaspoon ground black pepper

28 ⅓-inch-thick diagonal slices
    baguette, toasted
    Sour cream
    Caviar

Melt 3 tablespoons butter in heavy large skillet over medium heat. Add mushrooms and sauté until tender and beginning to brown, about 6 minutes. Mix in lemon peel. Set aside.

Whisk eggs, chives, salt and pepper in large bowl to blend. Melt 3 tablespoons butter in large nonstick skillet over medium heat. Add egg mixture and cook until eggs are softly set, stirring often, about 2 minutes. Mix in mushrooms.

Spoon egg mixture onto toasts. Top with sour cream and caviar. Transfer to platter and serve.

MAKING PERFECT OMELETS

Let's start with the pan. It's best to use a well-seasoned heavy pan or a nonstick one; if you are making an omelet for one person, a seven- to eight-inch skillet with angled sides is about the right size.

The key to producing a great omelet is to get the pan very hot before cooking. Place the empty pan over high heat for about one minute. To test whether the pan is hot enough, sprinkle a drop of water in the pan and make sure the drop "dances" across the pan.

When the pan has reached the proper temperature, add a little butter and then pour in the lightly beaten eggs. When the eggs begin to set, gently push them to the side with a fork, allowing the uncooked eggs to flow directly onto the pan's surface. This process should take less than one minute. If you're using a filling (such as cheese or mushrooms), now's the time to add it.

Before the eggs are completely set, shake the pan or use a spatula to loosen the omelet gently from the bottom and sides of the pan. Scoot the omelet so that its edge aligns with the left edge of the pan. Using the spatula, roll the right third of the omelet over the middle third. Tilt the pan so that the left edge of the pan is touching the plate, then turn the pan over, folding the omelet out of the pan and over onto itself on the plate.

HUEVOS RANCHEROS

This simple but highly seasoned breakfast, brunch or supper dish became fashionable during the craze for Tex-Mex food that began in the Southwest and California in the 1940s. Our recipe highlights tortillas that are currently available in a variety of flavors, like sun-dried tomato and jalapeño.

4 SERVINGS

¾ cup bottled salsa
1 medium plum tomato, chopped
3 tablespoons chopped fresh
    cilantro
4 tablespoons vegetable oil
4 7- to 9-inch flour or corn tortillas,
    flavored or plain

8 large eggs
1½ cups (packed) hot pepper
    Monterey Jack cheese (about
    6 ounces)

Preheat oven to 350°F. Mix first 3 ingredients in medium saucepan; set sauce aside. Heat 2 tablespoons oil in heavy large skillet over medium-high heat. Add 1 tortilla and cook until just beginning to brown, about 30 seconds. Using tongs, turn tortilla over and heat 10 seconds. Transfer to large sheet of foil. Repeat with remaining tortillas. Enclose tortillas in foil and place in oven to keep warm.

Divide remaining 2 tablespoons oil between 2 medium skillets and heat over medium heat. Break 4 eggs into each skillet; sprinkle with salt and pepper. Cook until just set on bottom, about 2 minutes. Sprinkle with cheese. Cover skillets; cook until eggs are cooked as desired and cheese melts, about 2 minutes. Bring sauce to boil.

Divide tortillas among 4 plates. Top each with 2 eggs, then warm sauce.

DOUBLE-SALMON AND SWEET POTATO HASH WITH POACHED EGGS

Herbs and a touch of maple syrup accent this colorful breakfast or brunch dish.

6 SERVINGS

¼ cup white wine vinegar
6 large eggs

4 tablespoons (½ stick) butter
2 pounds red-skinned sweet
    potatoes (yams), peeled, cut
    into ½-inch cubes
3 cups chopped leeks (white and
    pale green parts only)
1 large red bell pepper, diced
2 teaspoons dried thyme
1 12-ounce skinless salmon fillet,
    cut into ½-inch cubes
3 tablespoons pure maple syrup
2½ teaspoons chopped fresh sage
5 ounces thinly sliced smoked
    salmon, chopped

Paprika
Chopped fresh chives

Fill large bowl with cold water. Add enough water to large pot to measure 3 inches in depth; add vinegar and bring to simmer. Reduce heat to medium-low. Crack eggs open 1 at a time over simmering water and drop in. Poach eggs until whites are set, about 4 minutes. Using slotted spoon, transfer eggs to bowl of cold water to stop cooking; reserve pot of vinegar water.

Melt half of butter in each of 2 large nonstick skillets over low heat. Add half of sweet potatoes, leeks, bell pepper and thyme to each skillet; stir to coat with butter. Cover skillets; cook until potatoes are tender, stirring occasionally, about 8 minutes. Increase heat to medium-high. Uncover; cook without stirring until potatoes are golden on bottom, about 3 minutes. Using spatula, turn hash over in sections and cook without stirring until potatoes are gold-en on bottom, about 3 minutes longer. Fold half of fresh salmon, maple syrup and sage into hash in each skillet. Cook until salmon is just opaque in center, stirring occasionally, about 3 minutes. Mix half of smoked salmon into hash in each skillet. Season with salt and pepper. Remove from heat.

Meanwhile, bring reserved vinegar water to simmer; turn off heat. Transfer eggs to hot water 1 minute to rewarm.

Spoon hash onto plates. Remove eggs from water and place atop hash. Sprinkle with paprika and chives.

BUTTERMILK PANCAKES WITH BLUEBERRY COMPOTE

MAKES ABOUT 18

2½ cups all purpose flour
¼ cup sugar
2 teaspoons baking powder
2 teaspoons baking soda
1 teaspoon salt

2 cups buttermilk
2 cups sour cream
2 large eggs
4 teaspoons vanilla extract

3 tablespoons unsalted butter

Additional unsalted butter
Blueberry Compote (see recipe)

Whisk first 5 ingredients in large bowl. Whisk buttermilk, sour cream, eggs and vanilla in another large bowl. Add to dry ingredients. Stir until batter is just blend-ed but still lumpy (do not overmix).

Melt ½ tablespoon butter on griddle over medium heat. Pour batter by ⅓ cupfuls onto griddle, spacing 2 inches apart. Cook until bubbles break on surface, about 3 minutes. Turn pancakes over. Cook until bottoms are golden, 3 minutes. Transfer to plates. Repeat with remaining batter, adding butter to skillet as needed.

Serve pancakes immediately with butter and Blueberry Compote.

BLUEBERRY COMPOTE

MAKES ABOUT 1½ CUPS

2½ cups frozen blueberries, unthawed
⅓ cup sugar
⅓ cup water

Combine 1½ cups blueberries, sugar and ⅓ cup water in heavy small saucepan. Simmer over medium heat until berries burst, stirring often, about 10 minutes. Add remaining 1 cup berries. Cook until compote coats spoon, stirring often, about 8 minutes. (*Can be made 3 days ahead. Cover and chill.*) Serve warm.

A GOOD MIX

Making tender shortcakes (and coffee cakes and pancakes) is a breeze with the all-purpose baking mix from Beth's Basics. Organic flour is the secret to the fresh, light texture the mix produces. Call 800-425-2384.

ZUCCHINI-CURRANT PANCAKES

Aunt Jemima's Pancake Flour, first marketed in 1899, was America's original ready-mix food. Until the mix became nationally available in 1910, Americans thought of pancakes only as a hearty wintertime breakfast. But with the convenience offered by a mix, flapjacks were established as a quick anytime meal. Here, we've taken a few modern liberties with the favorite breakfast standby, with great results.

MAKES 12

2 cups all purpose flour
¼ cup sugar
1 teaspoon baking powder
1 teaspoon baking soda
½ teaspoon ground cinnamon
½ teaspoon ground allspice
½ teaspoon salt
1½ cups buttermilk
¾ cup vegetable oil
3 large eggs
1 medium zucchini, grated, squeezed to remove excess moisture
½ cup dried currants

Additional vegetable oil
Butter
Maple syrup

Preheat oven to 200°F. Whisk first 7 ingredients in large bowl. Whisk buttermilk, ¾ cup oil and eggs in medium bowl. Add to dry ingredients and mix just until blended but still lumpy. Fold in zucchini and currants.

Heat griddle or heavy large skillet over medium heat. Brush lightly with vegetable oil. Working in batches, pour batter by ⅓ cupfuls onto griddle, spacing apart. Cook until bottoms are golden, about 2 minutes. Turn and cook until second sides are golden and pancakes are cooked through, about 2 minutes. Transfer to baking sheet; keep warm in oven. Serve hot with butter and syrup.

Accompaniments

When you're really pressed for time, look no further than these easily prepared trimmings to make a meal extra-special. From vegetable dishes like Roasted Asparagus with Lemon or Dill Mashed Potatoes with Crëme Fraîche and Caviar to grains like Orzo Pilaf with Green Onions and Parmesan to such fresh-baked breads as Chili Cornmeal Muffins or Bacon and Thyme Biscuits, the recipes that follow are sure to result in a memorable menu.

Vegetables

Roasted Asparagus with Lemon

6 SERVINGS

3 tablespoons fresh lemon juice
1 tablespoon extra-virgin olive oil
1 teaspoon finely grated lemon peel
36 asparagus spears, trimmed

Preheat oven to 450°F. Mix lemon juice, oil and lemon peel in 15x10x2-inch glass baking dish. Add asparagus; turn to coat. Sprinkle with salt and pepper.

Roast asparagus until crisp-tender, turning occasionally, about 20 minutes. Serve warm or at room temperature.

Peas with Caraway, Black Pepper and Parmesan Butter

8 TO 10 SERVINGS

7 tablespoons freshly grated Parmesan cheese (about 1½ ounces)
6 tablespoons (¾ stick) butter, room temperature
1 teaspoon caraway seeds
¾ teaspoon grated lemon peel
½ teaspoon freshly cracked black pepper

¾ cup chopped shallots
3 10-ounce packages frozen petite peas, unthawed
⅓ cup canned beef broth or water
⅓ cup chopped fresh Italian parsley

Mix Parmesan cheese, 4 tablespoons butter, caraway seeds, lemon peel and pepper in small bowl. (*Can be prepared 3 days ahead. Cover and refrigerate.*)

Melt remaining 2 tablespoons butter in heavy large skillet over medium-high heat. Add shallots; sauté until tender, about 3 minutes. Add peas, broth and parsley and stir until peas are heated through, about 8 minutes. Add Parmesan butter and stir until melted. Season with salt. Transfer to bowl and serve.

BASIC STRAINING

With the set of KV&F colanders (one 8-inch, one 10-inch and one 12-inch), you can rinse lettuce and veggies and drain pasta, all at the same time. Available in black matte, chrome or titanium (dark gray). Call Savoir Vivre International at 212-684-6065.

SAUTÉED RADISHES AND SUGAR SNAP PEAS

12 SERVINGS

3½ pounds sugar snap peas, strings
  removed

6 tablespoons (¾ stick) butter
20 radishes (from 2 bunches),
  sliced ⅛ inch thick

Cook sugar snap peas in large pot of boiling salted water until crisp-tender, about 2 minutes. Drain. (*Can be prepared 1 day ahead. Wrap in paper towels. Place in sealable plastic bag and refrigerate.*)

Melt butter in heavy large pot over medium heat. Add radishes and sauté until translucent and crisp-tender, about 5 minutes. Add sugar snap peas. Sauté until peas are heated through, about 3 minutes. Season with salt and pepper.

Transfer vegetables to bowl; serve.

KEEPING COOKED VEGETABLES FRESH-LOOKING

A green vegetable's color starts to change after approximately six minutes of cooking. After ten minutes or so, the change is pronounced.

When preparing green vegetables, it's best to do as the French do: Cook them uncovered in a large pot of rapidly boiling salted water just until tender. Or micro-wave or quickly stir-fry the veggies.

Cooking is not the only thing that can discolor vegetables; acids in sauces and marinades can have the same effect. So if you plan to serve asparagus with lemon juice or broccoli with a vinaigrette, your best option is to put the dressing on right before serving.

CORN AND WINTER SQUASH WITH SPINACH AND BACON

A lovely dish that's a snap to prepare.

10 TO 12 SERVINGS

9 bacon slices, chopped
2 cups chopped onions
2½ pounds butternut squash, peeled,
  seeded, cut into ⅓-inch pieces
1½ 6-ounce packages baby spinach
  leaves
1 16-ounce package frozen corn
  kernels, thawed
6 tablespoons chopped fresh basil

Sauté bacon in large pot over medium heat until crisp, about 10 minutes. Add onions and squash. Sauté until squash is almost tender, about 12 minutes. Add spinach and corn. Toss until spinach wilts and corn is heated through, about 5 minutes. Stir in basil. Season with salt and pepper. Transfer to bowl and serve.

Green Beans and Red Bell Peppers with Marjoram and Almonds

Red peppers provide color and almonds provide crunch in this easy-to-make recipe.

8 TO 10 SERVINGS

2¼ pounds green beans, ends trimmed

5 tablespoons butter
3 large red bell peppers, thinly sliced
1 large onion, thinly sliced
¼ cup chopped fresh marjoram

¾ cup sliced almonds, toasted

Cook green beans in large pot of boiling salted water until just crisp-tender, about 5 minutes. Drain. Rinse with cold water. Drain well; set aside.

Melt 2 tablespoons butter in heavy large skillet over medium-high heat. Add peppers and onion and sauté until peppers are crisp-tender, about 8 minutes. Mix in marjoram. (*Beans and bell pepper mixture can be prepared 1 day ahead. Cover separately and refrigerate.*)

Melt remaining 3 tablespoons butter in heavy large pot over medium-high heat. Add beans and pepper mixture and stir until heated through, about 5 minutes. Season to taste with salt and pepper. Transfer to large bowl. Sprinkle with almonds.

Broccoli and Cauliflower with Lemon, Mustard and Chive Butter

The flavorful butter adds plenty of zip.

8 SERVINGS

½ cup (1 stick) butter, room temperature
2 tablespoons Dijon mustard
1 tablespoon grated lemon peel
⅓ cup plus 1 tablespoon chopped fresh chives

1 1½-pound whole cauliflower, trimmed, cut into florets
2½ pounds broccoli, stems trimmed, cut into florets

Using fork, blend butter, mustard and lemon peel in small bowl. Mix in ⅓ cup chives. Season with salt and pepper.

Cook cauliflower in large pot of boiling salted water 2 minutes. Add broccoli and cook until vegetables are crisp-tender, about 3 minutes longer. Drain. Transfer vegetables to bowl of ice water. Drain. (*Butter mixture and vegetables can be made 1 day ahead. Cover separately and chill.*)

Combine butter mixture and vegetables in large pot. Toss gently over medium heat until vegetables are heated through and coated with butter mixture, about 5 minutes. Transfer to bowl. Sprinkle with remaining 1 tablespoon chives.

BRUSSELS SPROUTS WITH GARLIC, PECANS AND BASIL

Lemon peel also enlivens this terrific dish.

6 TO 8 SERVINGS

1½ pounds small brussels sprouts, trimmed
¾ cup whipping cream
5 large garlic cloves, chopped

¾ cup pecans, toasted
¾ cup (packed) fresh basil leaves
1½ teaspoons grated lemon peel

Fresh basil sprigs (optional)
Lemon wedges (optional)

Combine brussels sprouts, cream and garlic in heavy large skillet. Bring to boil over medium-low heat. Cover skillet tightly and cook until brussels sprouts are crisp-tender but still bright green and almost all cream is absorbed, about 10 minutes.

Meanwhile, finely grind pecans with basil leaves and lemon peel in processor.

Add pecan mixture to skillet. Toss until brussels sprouts are coated. Season with salt and pepper. Transfer to serving bowl. Garnish with basil sprigs and lemon wedges, if desired, and serve.

RED CABBAGE WITH APRICOTS AND BALSAMIC VINEGAR

Here's a sweet-tart addition to your menu.

6 SERVINGS

6 tablespoons (¾ stick) butter
1 8-ounce red onion, thinly sliced
½ teaspoon ground allspice
¼ teaspoon ground nutmeg
1 1½-pound red cabbage, quartered, cored, very thinly sliced
¾ cup thinly sliced dried apricots
¼ cup apricot preserves
¼ cup balsamic vinegar

Melt butter in heavy large pot over medium-high heat. Add onion, allspice and nutmeg and toss 1 minute. Add cabbage and apricots and sauté until well coated, about 2 minutes. Add apricot preserves and vinegar and toss until juices are reduced to glaze and cabbage is crisp-tender, about 6 minutes. Season with salt and pepper. *(Can be prepared 1 day ahead. Cover and keep refrigerated. Rewarm over medium heat before serving.)*

Green Beans with Mushroom-Madeira Sauce

Remember the green bean casserole made with nothing but convenience ingredients: frozen or canned green beans, canned cream of mushroom soup and, for the topping, canned fried onions? Here it is again, only fresher and better.

6 SERVINGS

3 tablespoons butter
6 ounces shiitake mushrooms, stemmed and sliced
6 ounces oyster mushrooms, sliced
¾ teaspoon dried thyme
3 tablespoons chopped shallots
½ cup Madeira
1 cup whipping cream

1 pound fresh green beans, trimmed

Vegetable oil (for deep-frying)
2 large leeks (white and pale green parts only), thinly sliced crosswise

Melt 2 tablespoons butter in heavy large skillet over medium-high heat. Add all mushrooms and thyme; sauté 5 minutes. Add 2 tablespoons shallots; sauté until mushrooms are tender, about 3 minutes. Add Madeira and simmer until almost all liquid evaporates, about 2 minutes. Add cream and simmer until slightly thickened, about 2 minutes. Set sauce aside.

Cook beans in large pot of boiling salted water until just tender, 5 minutes. Drain. Transfer to bowl of ice water; cool. Drain. *(Sauce and beans can be made 6 hours ahead. Cover separately; chill.)*

Pour enough oil into large deep saucepan to reach depth of 4 inches. Heat oil to 350°F. Place ¼ of leeks in small metal strainer. Lower strainer into oil; fry until golden, 40 seconds. Lift strainer from oil. Drain leeks on paper towels. Repeat with remaining leeks in 3 more batches. Season leeks with salt.

Melt 1 tablespoon butter in heavy large skillet over medium heat. Add beans and remaining 1 tablespoon shallots; toss to heat through. Season with salt and pepper. Place beans on platter.

Bring sauce to simmer. Spoon sauce over beans. Sprinkle with fried leeks.

Roasted Vegetables with Garlic-Tarragon Butter

A delicious and colorful dish that can be made any time of year.

6 SERVINGS

2 medium-size red onions, cut into ½-inch-thick rounds
2 red bell peppers, quartered lengthwise, seeded
4 zucchini or yellow crookneck squash, cut on diagonal into ½-inch-thick slices
2 large portobello mushrooms, dark gills scraped away, quartered

1 head radicchio, cut into 6 wedges
6 tablespoons (¾ stick) butter
6 small garlic cloves, minced
2 teaspoons dried tarragon
3 tablespoons dry white wine
1 tablespoon olive oil

Lemon wedges

Position 1 rack in top third and 1 rack in bottom third of oven and preheat to 500°F. Arrange vegetables in single layer on 2 large baking sheets. Stir butter, garlic and tarragon in heavy small saucepan over low heat until butter melts. Whisk in wine and oil. Brush vegetables with all of butter mixture; sprinkle generously with salt and pepper.

Roast vegetables 10 minutes. Turn vegetables over, reverse position of baking sheets and roast until vegetables are tender and browned in spots, about 10 minutes longer. Transfer vegetables to large platter. Serve with lemon wedges.

Potatoes

MASHED POTATOES WITH PROSCIUTTO AND PARMESAN CHEESE
Here are potatoes with Italian flavor.

8 SERVINGS

3¼ pounds russet potatoes, peeled, cut into 1-inch pieces
4 large garlic cloves, peeled

½ cup (1 stick) butter
3½ ounces thinly sliced prosciutto, finely chopped
¾ teaspoon minced fresh rosemary

¾ cup (or more) whole milk
1 cup freshly grated Parmesan cheese (about 3 ounces)

Additional fresh rosemary

Cook potatoes and garlic in large pot of boiling salted water until potatoes are very tender, about 15 minutes. Drain; return potatoes and garlic to same pot.

Meanwhile, melt ½ cup butter in heavy small saucepan over medium heat. Add chopped prosciutto and ¾ teaspoon minced rosemary and sauté until fragrant, about 2 minutes.

Add prosciutto mixture and ¾ cup milk to potatoes and garlic. Mash well, adding more milk by tablespoonfuls if potatoes are dry. Mix in ¾ cup cheese. Season with salt and pepper. *(Can be prepared 6 hours ahead. Cover and chill. Stir over low heat to rewarm, adding more milk by tablespoonfuls, if desired.)*

Transfer potatoes to bowl. Sprinkle with remaining ¼ cup cheese; garnish with fresh rosemary and serve.

minutes. Drain. Return potatoes to pot and mash. Add chive mixture, buttermilk and remaining 3 tablespoons butter and mash together. Season with salt and pepper.

MASHED POTATOES WITH LEMON AND CHIVES

4 SERVINGS

6 tablespoons (¾ stick) butter
2 garlic cloves, minced
2 teaspoons grated lemon peel
½ cup chopped fresh chives

2 pounds russet potatoes, cut
    into 1-inch pieces
¼ cup buttermilk

Melt 3 tablespoons butter in heavy small skillet over medium heat. Add garlic and sauté 1 minute. Mix in lemon peel, then chives. Set aside.

Cook potatoes in large pot of boiling salted water until tender, about 20

MAKE MASHED POTATOES AHEAD? YES, YOU CAN.

The turkey is ready, the dressing is steaming, the gravy is just right—and it's taking longer to mash the potatoes than you had planned. Guess what? This essential element of a holiday feast can be made ahead.

To do so, simply mash (or mix, as you prefer) the potatoes as usual, then cover them with plastic wrap and store them in the refrigerator for up to six hours. At serving time, reheat the potatoes in a microwave oven or a large saucepan over medium heat, adding a little milk or broth as necessary to achieve the desired consistency and stirring occasionally. (A caution: Water tends to dilute the potatoes, and cream can make them too thick.) With your do-ahead potatoes at the ready, there's one less thing to worry about at the last minute.

DILL MASHED POTATOES WITH CRÈME FRAÎCHE AND CAVIAR

Crème fraîche makes these potatoes extra rich and utterly delicious.

6 TO 8 SERVINGS

3½ pounds russet potatoes, peeled, cut into 2-inch pieces
1 cup crème fraîche or sour cream
¼ cup (½ stick) butter, room temperature
3 tablespoons (packed) finely chopped fresh dill

1 4-ounce jar salmon caviar

Cook potatoes in large pot of boiling salted water until very tender, about 25 minutes. Drain well. Return potatoes to pot; mash over low heat until almost smooth. Add crème fraîche and butter; whisk until smooth and fluffy. Stir in dill. Season with salt and pepper. (*Potatoes can be made 2 hours ahead. Cover and let stand at room temperature. Rewarm over low heat, stirring frequently.*)

Top potatoes with caviar and serve.

YAMS BRAISED WITH CREAM, ROSEMARY AND NUTMEG

Simmering the yams fills them with flavor and yields a lovely coating.

8 SERVINGS

4 teaspoons olive oil
½ cup finely chopped shallots
2½ teaspoons minced fresh rosemary
3 pounds yams (red-skinned sweet potatoes), peeled, cut into ½-inch-thick rounds, rounds cut in half
1¼ cups canned low-salt chicken broth
½ cup whipping cream
Ground nutmeg

Heat oil in heavy large skillet over medium-high heat. Add shallots and minced rosemary and sauté until tender, about 3 minutes. Add yams and broth to skillet and bring to boil. Cover skillet, reduce heat to medium-low and simmer until yams are almost tender, about 10 minutes. Add cream and sprinkle lightly with nutmeg. Simmer uncovered until yams are very tender and liquid thickens and coats yams, about 4 minutes. Season with salt and pepper. (*Can be made 1 day ahead. Transfer to microwave-safe dish. Chill until cold, then cover and keep chilled. Rewarm, covered, in microwave on medium-low heat.*)

ARE YAMS AND SWEET POTATOES THE SAME THING OR NOT?

No, they're not the same. Sweet potatoes and yams actually come from different families, but most people (and markets) now use the two names interchangeably.

In fact, it's unlikely that the vegetables you serve at your Thanksgiving dinner are true yams. In this country those tubers are usually found only in certain ethnic markets. Native to Asia and Africa, yams have thick skin, and the sweet flesh can be white, orange or purple.

Sweet potatoes, however, are widely available in two varieties. One has tan skin and dry yellow flesh with a flavor reminiscent of chestnuts. The darker-skinned variety has sweet orange flesh and is the type that is often mistakenly labeled in supermarkets as a yam.

The darker variety of sweet potato can be substituted for yams in many recipes, while the lighter variety of sweet potato will sometimes work in place of regular potatoes.

INDIAN POTATOES, PEAS AND CAULIFLOWER

4 SERVINGS

2 tablespoons vegetable oil
1 pound russet potatoes, peeled, cut into ½-inch pieces
1 tablespoon minced fresh ginger
4 cups cauliflower florets, cut into bite-size pieces
½ teaspoon salt
½ teaspoon ground turmeric
¼ teaspoon chili powder
¼ teaspoon paprika
½ cup water
½ cup frozen peas, thawed

Heat oil in large nonstick skillet over medium heat. Add potatoes and ginger; sauté until potatoes are lightly browned, about 3 minutes. Mix in cauliflower, then salt, turmeric, chili powder and paprika; sauté 5 minutes.

Add ½ cup water; cover and simmer until vegetables are tender, about 5 minutes. Add peas and simmer 2 minutes. Season with salt and pepper.

Grains

ORZO PILAF WITH GREEN ONIONS AND PARMESAN CHEESE

The rice-shaped pasta orzo is sometimes labeled riso or rosamarina.

6 SERVINGS

3¼ cups (or more) canned low-salt chicken broth
1 pound orzo (rice-shaped pasta)
5 green onions, thinly sliced
¾ cup grated Parmesan cheese

Bring 3¼ cups broth to boil in heavy large saucepan over medium-high heat. Mix in orzo and simmer uncovered until just tender but still firm to bite and some broth still remains, stirring occasionally, about 8 minutes. Remove from heat. Add green onions and cheese and stir to blend. Season pilaf to taste with salt and pepper. Rewarm over low heat, if necessary, and mix in more broth by ¼ cupfuls if pilaf is dry. Transfer pilaf to large bowl and serve.

SZECHUAN SESAME NOODLES

Spicy Szechuan dishes were quite the thing in the seventies; around that time, pasta was also coming into its own. This recipe features ingredients that are widely available in the Asian foods section of most markets. If you like, add snow peas and sliced red bell pepper for some crunch.

6 SIDE-DISH SERVINGS

8 ounces thin dried Asian noodles or linguine
4 tablespoons oriental sesame oil
3 tablespoons chopped peanuts
2 tablespoons finely chopped peeled fresh ginger
3 large garlic cloves, minced
6 tablespoons bottled teriyaki sauce
2 tablespoons fresh lime juice
1 teaspoon chili-garlic sauce
1½ cups thinly sliced green or red onions

Cook noodles in large pot of boiling salted water until tender but still firm to bite. Drain; return noodles to same pot. Mix in 1 tablespoon oil and peanuts.

Heat 3 tablespoons oil in heavy small skillet over medium-low heat. Add ginger and garlic; stir 10 seconds. Add teriyaki sauce, lime juice and chili sauce; simmer 30 seconds. Mix sauce and onions into noodles. Season with salt and pepper. Serve warm or at room temperature.

POLENTA WITH FRESH HERBS AND WHITE CHEDDAR CHEESE

Regarded as peasant food for centuries, polenta achieved culinary stardom in the past few years, thanks to widespread exploration of all aspects of Italian gastronomy. Polenta can be enjoyed in its soft, creamy state right after being prepared; or it can be chilled in a loaf pan, sliced and cooked on a grill or griddle. Try this soft version with sausages. The coarse polenta specified is sometimes labeled "stone-ground corn grits."

6 SIDE-DISH SERVINGS

6⅔ cups canned low-salt chicken broth
 2 teaspoons minced fresh marjoram
 2 teaspoons minced fresh thyme
 2 teaspoons minced fresh sage
 1 garlic clove, minced
 1 teaspoon salt
1⅔ cups polenta (coarse cornmeal)*
1½ cups (packed) grated sharp white cheddar cheese (about 6 ounces)

Combine broth, all herbs, garlic and salt in heavy large saucepan and bring to boil over medium-high heat. Gradually sprinkle in polenta, whisking constantly. Reduce heat to medium-low; simmer until polenta is thick and creamy and begins to pull away from sides of pan, whisking often, about 25 minutes. Add cheese; stir until cheese melts. Season with salt and pepper and serve.

*Sold at Italian markets, natural foods stores and some supermarkets. If unavailable, use 1⅔ cups regular cornmeal and cook for about 12 minutes.

Breads
OLD-FASHIONED CORN BREAD

12 SERVINGS

1¼ cups yellow cornmeal
 ¾ cup all purpose flour
 2 teaspoons baking soda
 ½ teaspoon salt
 1 cup whole milk
 1 large egg, beaten to blend
 3 tablespoons butter, melted

Preheat oven to 375°F. Lightly butter 8½-inch square baking pan. Stir cornmeal, flour, baking soda and salt in large bowl. Add milk, egg and butter; stir just to blend. Pour batter into prepared pan.

Bake corn bread until tester inserted into center comes out clean and top is golden brown, about 20 minutes. Transfer pan to rack and cool.

GARLIC BREAD WITH PECORINO ROMANO BUTTER

10 SERVINGS

½ cup (1 stick) unsalted butter, room temperature
½ cup grated pecorino Romano cheese
¼ cup finely chopped fresh Italian parsley
2 garlic cloves, minced

1 14-inch-long loaf Italian or French bread, halved lengthwise

Mix butter, cheese, parsley and garlic in medium bowl to blend well. Season with pepper. (*Can be prepared 1 day ahead. Cover and refrigerate. Bring to room temperature before using.*)

Preheat oven to 500°F. Place bread, cut side up, on baking sheet. Spread butter mixture evenly over cut sides of bread. Bake until topping is golden brown and bread is heated through, about 5 minutes.

Cut bread crosswise into 2-inch-wide pieces. Serve immediately.

CHILI CORNMEAL MUFFINS

Corn kernels and chili powder lend a southwestern accent to these muffins. They would be nice alongside a bowl of chili.

MAKES 12

½ cup (1 stick) unsalted butter
1 cup frozen corn kernels, thawed
4 teaspoons chili powder
1 cup buttermilk
2 large eggs

1 cup yellow cornmeal
1 cup all purpose flour
3 tablespoons sugar
2 teaspoons baking powder
1 teaspoon salt
½ teaspoon baking soda

Preheat oven to 400°F. Butter twelve ⅓-cup metal muffin cups. Melt butter in heavy medium skillet over medium heat. Add corn and chili powder. Sauté 3 minutes. Transfer to medium bowl. Mix in buttermilk, then eggs. Cool completely.

Whisk cornmeal, flour, sugar, baking powder, salt and baking soda in large bowl to blend. Add buttermilk mixture; stir just until blended.

Divide batter among prepared muffin cups. Bake until tester inserted into center of muffins comes out clean, about 20 minutes. Transfer muffins to rack. Cool slightly. (*Can be made 2 weeks ahead. Cool completely. Wrap in foil, seal in plastic bag and freeze. Rewarm muffins wrapped in foil in 350°F oven until heated through, about 8 minutes.*)

Baked Baguette with Lemon-Garlic Butter

Lemon peel gives extra zip to this warm, garlicky bread. The recipe makes enough for everyone to have more than one helping.

6 SERVINGS

½ cup (1 stick) butter, room temperature
2 tablespoons chopped fresh parsley
3 garlic cloves, pressed
1 teaspoon grated lemon peel
1 French-bread baguette, cut crosswise into 1-inch-thick slices

Mix butter, chopped parsley, garlic and grated lemon peel in small bowl to blend. Season lemon-garlic butter to taste with salt and pepper. Spread evenly over 1 side of each bread slice. Reassemble bread slices; wrap in foil. Place on baking sheet. (*Can be made 8 hours ahead; chill.*)

Preheat oven to 300°F. Bake bread until heated through, about 20 minutes; serve bread warm.

Bacon and Thyme Biscuits

MAKES 8

4 bacon slices, chopped

2⅓ cups all purpose flour
4 teaspoons baking powder
1 tablespoon sugar
1 teaspoon dried thyme
¾ teaspoon salt
½ teaspoon baking soda
½ cup chilled solid vegetable shortening, cut into pieces
¾ cup buttermilk

Melted butter

Preheat oven to 400°F. Cook bacon in heavy large skillet over medium heat until crisp, about 4 minutes. Using slotted spoon, transfer bacon to paper towels and drain. Reserve 2 tablespoons bacon drippings.

Mix flour, baking powder, sugar, dried thyme, salt and baking soda in large bowl. Add chilled shortening; cut in until mixture resembles coarse meal. Add buttermilk, reserved bacon drippings and chopped bacon; stir until mixture is just combined. Gather dough together. Turn dough out onto lightly floured surface and knead several turns until smooth. Pat out dough to 8-inch round. Cut round into 8 wedges. Transfer wedges to baking sheet, spacing 2 inches apart.

Bake biscuits until puffed and golden, about 18 minutes. Brush tops with melted butter. Cool slightly. (*Can be made 1 day ahead. Cool completely. Wrap in foil; let stand at room temperature. Rewarm in 350°F oven until heated through, about 5 minutes.*) Serve warm.

Green Onion Biscuits

MAKES 16

3 cups all purpose flour
1½ tablespoons baking powder

1½ teaspoons salt
1 teaspoon freshly ground black
  pepper
2⅓ cups chilled whipping cream
1½ cups thinly sliced green onions

2 tablespoons (¼ stick) butter,
  melted

Preheat oven to 425°F. Mix flour, baking powder, salt and pepper in large bowl. Mix cream and green onions in medium bowl. Add cream mixture to dry ingredients. Stir until moist clumps form.

Transfer dough to floured work surface. Knead just until dough holds together, about 8 turns. Shape into 8-inch square. Cut out sixteen 2-inch square biscuits. Transfer biscuits to large baking sheet, spacing 1½ inches apart. Brush top of biscuits with melted butter.

Bake biscuits until golden and cooked through, about 18 minutes. Serve warm. (*Can be made 8 hours ahead. Cool. Wrap in foil. Store at room temperature. Rewarm wrapped biscuits in 350°F oven until heated through, about 8 minutes.*)

DOUBLE-CORN AND CHEESE MUFFINS

Jiffy muffin mixes were part of the boxed baking craze that took hold in the thirties, and they remain a supermarket staple. Here, frozen corn kernels, shredded cheese and fresh basil are convenient additions.

MAKES 8

⅓ cup whole milk
1 large egg
1 8½-ounce box corn muffin mix
⅓ cup (packed) shredded "pizza
  cheese" or mozzarella cheese
⅓ cup frozen corn kernels, thawed
3 tablespoons chopped fresh basil

Preheat oven to 400°F. Line eight ⅓-cup muffin cups with paper liners.

Blend milk and egg in small bowl. Place remaining ingredients in large bowl; add milk mixture. Stir until ingredients are just moistened (do not overmix). Divide batter among prepared muffin cups.

Bake muffins until golden and tester inserted into center comes out clean, about 20 minutes. Serve muffins warm.

SCOTTISH OATCAKES

These slightly sweet rounds are a cross between a cookie and a cracker. Eat them plain or with jam for breakfast, or top them with cheese for a snack.

MAKES ABOUT 18

1½ cups old-fashioned oats
1 cup all purpose flour
½ cup sugar
½ teaspoon baking soda
¼ teaspoon salt
½ cup chilled solid vegetable
  shortening, cut into pieces
¼ cup buttermilk

Preheat oven to 350°F. Butter 2 heavy large baking sheets. Place oats in large bowl. Sift flour, sugar, baking soda and salt into same bowl. Using fingertips, rub in shortening until mixture resembles coarse meal. Add buttermilk; stir until dough forms. Transfer dough to floured surface. Roll out dough to ¼-inch thickness. Using 2½-inch round cookie cutter, cut out rounds. Arrange on prepared sheets, spacing apart. Gather scraps, reroll and cut out additional rounds.

Bake oatcakes until edges are pale golden, about 12 minutes. Transfer baking sheets to racks and cool 5 minutes. Transfer cakes to racks; cool completely. *(Can be prepared 3 days ahead. Store in airtight container at room temperature.)*

FIVE-MINUTE SPICED ORANGE MARMALADE

Honey, brandy and spices enhance purchased marmalade for an easy-to-make spread for breads.

MAKES ABOUT 3 CUPS
(ENOUGH FOR THREE 8-OUNCE JARS)

½ cup honey
½ cup brandy
3 cinnamon sticks
3 whole star anise*
1 vanilla bean, cut crosswise into
  3 pieces
3 3x1-inch strips orange peel
  (orange part only)

12 whole cloves
2 14- to 16-ounce jars orange
  marmalade

Combine first 5 ingredients in large saucepan. Pierce each orange peel strip with 4 cloves, spacing apart; add to pan. Simmer until mixture is reduced to ½ cup, about 5 minutes. Add marmalade; bring to simmer, stirring often. Remove from heat.

Using tongs, transfer 1 star anise, 1 cinnamon stick, 1 vanilla piece and 1 orange-clove strip to each of three 8-ounce canning jars. Fill each jar with hot marmalade and seal with lids. *(Can be prepared 4 weeks ahead. Refrigerate.)*

*Brown star-shaped seed pods sold at Asian markets and specialty foods stores and in the spice section of some supermarkets.

BAKING SHEET BUYER'S CHECKLIST

Always buy heavy-duty baking sheets; aluminum ones are best.

In general, get large sheets and baking pans, and stock your pantry with more than one of each.

Avoid black-metal sheets. They can burn cookies quickly.

Line sheets with silicone-coated parchment paper before using.

Desserts

Often, the quickest, most delicious dessert of all is a selection of fresh fruit. Not surprisingly, then, seasonal produce figures prominently in the recipes that follow, from Strawberry and Macaroon Parfaits to Triple-Cherries Jubilee to Red, White and Blue Ice Cream Sundaes. You may be surprised, however, by how easily you can make desserts that seem more complicated, such as Flourless Peanut Butter and Chocolate Chip Cookies, Caramel-Cognac Fondue and Tiramisù Angel Cake Torte.

Fruit

FRESH FRUIT SALAD WITH HONEY, MINT AND LIME SYRUP

A refreshing dessert on its own or spooned over vanilla ice cream.

8 SERVINGS

¼ cup fresh lime juice
¼ cup honey
¼ cup chopped fresh mint
1 3-pound cantaloupe, halved, seeded
1 12-ounce basket strawberries, hulled, halved
4 kiwis, peeled, cut into ½-inch pieces
1½ cups seedless grapes

Whisk lime juice, honey and mint in large bowl to blend. Using melon baller, scoop out cantaloupe. Add all fruit to syrup in bowl; toss to combine. Let stand 15 minutes to allow flavors to blend. (*Can be made 3 hours ahead. Cover and chill.*) Spoon fruit into goblets.

STRAWBERRY AND MACAROON PARFAITS

This pretty dessert calls for purchased macaroons; that's why it's so easy to prepare.

4 SERVINGS

2 cups sliced hulled strawberries (about 12 ounces)
1 10-ounce package frozen strawberries in syrup, thawed
1½ cups coarsely crushed Italian-style almond macaroons or crushed almond biscotti
1 pint vanilla frozen yogurt
4 additional strawberries (optional)

Mix sliced strawberries and strawberries in syrup in medium bowl. Divide half of strawberry mixture among four 10- to 12-ounce goblets or wineglasses. Top with half of macaroons and small scoops of frozen yogurt. Repeat layering. Top each with 1 fresh strawberry, if desired.

CARAMEL-COGNAC FONDUE

This indulgent Cognac-spiked dessert fondue is perfect for a romantic evening by the fire.

4 SERVINGS

½ cup sugar
2 tablespoons water

1⅓ cups warm whipping cream
2 tablespoons Cognac
1 tablespoon unsalted butter

Fresh strawberries, thinly sliced apples or pears, sliced bananas, fresh tangerine segments and sliced star fruit

Combine sugar and 2 tablespoons water in heavy medium saucepan. Stir over low heat until sugar dissolves. Increase heat; boil without stirring until mixture is deep amber color, occasionally brushing down sides of pan with wet pastry brush and swirling pan, about 3 minutes.

Add warm cream to caramel. Stir over medium-high heat until sauce is smooth and reduced to 1¼ cups, about 5 minutes. Add Cognac and cook 1 minute longer. Remove from heat. Add butter and stir until melted. (*Can be prepared 8 hours ahead. Cover and chill. Rewarm over medium-low heat before serving.*)

Transfer sauce to small fondue pot or flameproof ceramic bowl. Set pot over candle or canned heat burner. Serve with strawberries, apples or pears, bananas, tangerine segments and star fruit.

Ice Cream & Parfaits

TRIPLE-CHERRIES JUBILEE

Flaming desserts—like this one and crepes suzette—were all the rage at fine dining establishments in the sixties. The title here refers to the sweet cherries, dried cherries and cherry juice—enhanced by vanilla bean and orange peel—that provide such terrific flavor.

6 SERVINGS

1 1-pound bag frozen dark sweet cherries, thawed
2 cups plus 1 tablespoon cherry juice
½ cup dried tart cherries

3 tablespoons sugar
1 vanilla bean, split lengthwise
1 tablespoon arrowroot
¼ cup thin matchstick-size strips orange peel (orange part only)

⅓ cup kirsch (clear cherry brandy)
1 quart vanilla or cherry-vanilla-swirl ice cream

Place sieve over bowl. Add thawed cherries; let drain. Pour drained juices into heavy medium skillet (set cherries aside). Mix 2 cups cherry juice, dried cherries and sugar into same skillet. Scrape in seeds from vanilla bean; add bean. Boil sauce until reduced to 1½ cups, stirring occasionally, about 12 minutes.

Mix arrowroot with remaining 1 tablespoon juice in small bowl. Whisk into sauce. Boil until thickened, about 1 minute. Discard vanilla bean. Mix in drained cherries and orange peel.Heat kirsch in skillet over low heat. Remove from heat. Carefully ignite kirsch with match. Carefully pour flaming kirsch into sauce. Scoop ice cream into bowls. Spoon sauce over.

RED, WHITE AND BLUE ICE CREAM SUNDAES

Strawberry sauce and fresh blueberries and strawberries are the colorful toppers for vanilla ice cream.

8 SERVINGS

3 16-ounce baskets strawberries, hulled, quartered
1 16-ounce package frozen sliced sweetened strawberries, thawed
½ cup seedless raspberry jam

1 quart vanilla ice cream
2 1-pint baskets blueberries

Purée 1 basket strawberries, thawed strawberries and jam in processor. Pour sauce into bowl. (*Can be made 4 hours ahead. Cover and chill.*)

Scoop ice cream into 8 bowls. Serve with sauce, blueberries and remaining 2 baskets quartered strawberries.

COFFEE-CARAMEL SAUCE

For a nice gift, simply decorate the jars with gold ribbon, and attach tags that include the rewarming instructions.

MAKES ABOUT 1¾ CUPS (ENOUGH FOR TWO 8-OUNCE JARS)

8 tablespoons water
4 teaspoons instant coffee powder
1⅓ cups sugar
⅔ cup whipping cream
5 tablespoons unsalted butter, diced
Pinch of salt

Stir 2 tablespoons water and 4 teaspoons coffee powder in small bowl until coffee powder dissolves. Stir remaining 6 tablespoons water and 1⅓ cups sugar in heavy medium saucepan over low heat until sugar dissolves. Increase heat and boil without

stirring until syrup turns deep amber, occasionally brushing down sides of pan with pastry brush dipped into water and swirling pan, about 8 minutes. Remove saucepan from heat. Add whipping cream, butter and coffee mixture (mixture will bubble vigorously). Return to heat and bring to boil, whisking constantly until smooth. Whisk in salt. Divide sauce between two 8-ounce canning jars; seal jars tightly with lids. (*Sauce can be prepared 2 weeks ahead; refrigerate. Rewarm over medium-low heat, stirring constantly.*)

OH, FUDGE!

It's hard to resist Susan Elaine's Incredibly Decadent dessert sauces. For a 9.75-ounce jar of rich bittersweet chocolate, mocha or espresso flavor, call 310-476-5341 to order.

Baked Goods

FLOURLESS PEANUT BUTTER AND CHOCOLATE CHIP COOKIES

A couple of the best convenience foods of the century undoubtedly are peanut butter (introduced at the 1904 St. Louis World's Fair) and chocolate chips (first sold by Nestlé in 1939). Separately, they are the basis of two of the nation's favorite cookies. Together, the ingredients are an unbeatable team.

MAKES ABOUT 24

1 cup super chunky peanut butter
1 cup (packed) golden brown sugar
1 large egg
1 teaspoon baking soda
½ teaspoon vanilla extract
1 cup miniature semisweet
    chocolate chips (about 6 ounces)

Preheat oven to 350°F. Mix first 5 ingredients in medium bowl. Mix in chocolate chips. Using moistened hands, form generous 1 tablespoon dough for each cookie into ball. Arrange on 2 ungreased baking sheets, spacing 2 inches apart.

Bake cookies until puffed, golden on bottom and still soft to touch in center, about 12 minutes. Cool on sheets 5 minutes. Transfer to racks; cool completely.

MOCHA-CHIP COOKIES

MAKES ABOUT 4½ DOZEN

1¼ cups all purpose flour
1 cup whole wheat flour
1 tablespoon baking soda
1 cup (2 sticks) unsalted butter,
    room temperature
¾ cup sugar
¾ cup (packed) golden brown sugar
2 large eggs
2 teaspoons instant coffee powder
2 teaspoons vanilla extract
1 12-ounce package semisweet
    chocolate chips
1 cup chopped toasted walnuts

Preheat oven to 375°F. Mix both flours and baking soda in medium bowl. Using electric mixer, beat butter and both sugars in large bowl until light. Beat in eggs, coffee powder and vanilla. Beat in flour mixture. Stir in chocolate chips and nuts. Drop dough by tablespoonfuls onto ungreased baking sheets, spacing 2 inches apart. Bake until golden brown but still soft, about 9 minutes. Cool on sheets 2 minutes. Transfer to racks and cool.

EASY DOUGH

Making cookies couldn't be simpler with the pre-mixed, pre-shaped dough from Tom's. One-pound tubs are available in five irresistible flavors: chocolate chip, snickerdoodle, peanut butter-chocolate chip, *caffè latte* and oatmeal-raisin. Call 415-989-8667 for stores.

TIRAMISÙ ANGEL CAKE TORTE

Loosely translated, tiramisù means "pick me up," and it has been picked up on practically every menu in America. Since the early eighties, it has been one of the most famous Italian-American desserts, and like spaghetti and meatballs, it is far more prevalent here than in Italy. Purchased angel food cake makes this especially easy.

8 TO 10 SERVINGS

- 8 ounces Philadelphia-brand cream cheese, room temperature
- 2 cups chilled whipping cream
- ⅔ cup powdered sugar
- 6 tablespoons amaretto
- 3 tablespoons unsweetened cocoa powder
- 1 tablespoon instant espresso powder or coffee powder
- 1 9- to 10-inch angel food cake
- 3 ounces bittersweet (not unsweetened) or semisweet chocolate, coarsely grated
- 1 cup sliced almonds, toasted
  Chocolate shavings (optional)

Using electric mixer, beat cream cheese in large bowl until smooth. Add 1 cup whipping cream, ⅔ cup powdered sugar, 2 tablespoons amaretto, cocoa and espresso powder. Beat until fluffy and smooth. Using same beaters, beat remaining 1 cup cream in medium bowl until firm peaks form. Fold whipped cream into cheese mixture for frosting.

Cut cake horizontally into 3 equal layers. Place bottom cake layer on platter. Sprinkle with 4 teaspoons amaretto. Spread with 1 cup frosting. Sprinkle with half of grated chocolate. Repeat layering with cake, amaretto, frosting and grated chocolate. Top with third cake layer. Sprinkle with 4 teaspoons amaretto. Spread remaining frosting over cake. Press almonds onto sides of cake. Top with chocolate shavings, if desired.

INDEX

Appetizers
  Artichoke Bruschetta, 7
  Asparagus and Sugar Snap Peas with Honey-
    Mustard Dip, 2
  Beef and Broccoli Wontons with Ginger
    Dipping Sauce, 11
  Blue Cheese Dip with Pecans, 3
  Butter Bean and Cumin Hummus, 5-6
  Caesar Dip with Crudités, 2
  Camembert with Blue Cheese, Figs and
    Port Sauce, 4
  Chicken and Mushroom Quesadillas, 13
  Crostini with Gorgonzola and Figs, 6-7
  Crudités with Asian-Style Dip, 4
  Deviled Eggs with Curry, 8
  Grilled Bread Topped with Arugula, Goat Cheese,
    Olives and Onions, 3
  Red Caviar Dip, 6
  Risotto with Spicy Sausage, 12
  Scallops and Leeks in Star Anise-Orange
    Sauce, 10
  Smoked-Salmon Pizza with Red Onion
    and Dill, 10
  Smoked Salmon Tartare with Ginger and
    Sesame, 9
  Smoked Salmon with Sour Cream-Caper Sauce, 7
  Sugar and Spice Pepitas, 9-10
  Sweet and Spicy Candied Pecans, 13

Apple(s)
  Cider, Hot, with Ginger and Cardamom, 18
  Smoked Trout, Watercress and Apple Salad with
    Creamy Horseradish Dressing, 32
  Waldorf Salad, 29-30
Artichoke(s)
  Bruschetta, 7
  Lima Bean and Pea Salad, 28
  Olives and Feta, Flatbread Pizzas with, 66
Arugula
  Grilled Bread Topped with Arugula, Goat Cheese,
    Olives and Onions, 3
  Mayonnaise, Smoked-Turkey Tea Sandwiches
    with, 63
  Salad, Veal Chops with, 48-49
  Winter Greens with Grapefruit Vinaigrette, 23
Asparagus
  Roasted, with Lemon, 74
  Shrimp and Sun-Dried Tomatoes, Penne with, 60
  and Sugar Snap Peas with Honey-Mustard Dip, 2
Avocado(s)
  Mexican-Style Chicken Sandwiches, 68
  Salad Bar Cobb, 33

Bacon
  The Best BLTs, 61
  and Spinach, with Corn and Winter Squash, 75

  and Thyme Biscuits, 86
Banana, Peanut Butter and Date Sandwiches, 64
Bean(s)
  Black Bean and Vegetable Wraps, 65-66
  Butter Bean and Cumin Hummus, 5-6
  Mexican-Style Chicken Sandwiches, 68
  Quick Black Bean Soup, 20-21
Beef
  and Broccoli Wontons with Ginger Dipping
    Sauce, 11
  Hamburgers with Mustard and Mixed Herbs, 62
  Medallions with Cognac Sauce, 46
  Rib-Eye Steaks with Bérnaise Butter, 45
  and Sausage Tacos, Spicy, 66-67
  Sirloin Patties with Vegetable Sauce, 46-47
  Tenderloin with Garlic and Brandy, 46
Beet Salad, Country, 28-29
Bell Pepper(s), Red
  and Broiled Fennel Salad, 25
  and Green Beans with Marjoram and Almonds, 76
  Mushroom and Squash Salad, 23
  Roasted Vegetables with Garlic-Tarragon
    Butter, 78-79
  Spicy Beef and Sausage Tacos, 66-67
Beverages
  Blended Citrus Gin Fizz, 17
  Candy Cane Hot White Chocolate, 18
  French 75 Cocktail, 16

Hot Apple Cider with Ginger and Cardamom, 18
Hot Cocoa with Coffee Liqueur, 14
Kir Vodka Martinis, 14
Mango-Boysenberry Mimosa, 15
Southwestern Bloody Mary, 16
Biscuits
  Bacon and Thyme, 86
  Green Onion, 86-87
Blueberry Compote, 72
Boysenberry-Mango Mimosa, 15
Bread(s)
  Artichoke Bruschetta, 7
  Bacon and Thyme Biscuits, 86
  Baked Baguette with Lemon-Garlic Butter, 86
  Bruschetta, Artichoke, 7
  Corn Bread, Old-Fashioned, 84
  Crostini with Gorgonzola and Figs, 6-7
  Double-Corn and Cheese Muffins, 87
  Garlic Bread with Pecorino Romano Butter, 85
  Grilled, Topped with Arugula, Goat Cheese,
    Olives and Onions, 3
  Parmesan Toasts, 22-23
  Scottish Oatcakes, 87-88
Broccoli
  and Beef Wontons with Ginger Dipping Sauce, 11
  and Cauliflower with Lemon, Mustard and
    Chive Butter, 76
Brussels Sprouts with Garlic, Pecans and Basil, 77

Cabbage
  Red Cabbage with Apricots and Balsamic
    Vinegar, 77
Caesar Dip with Crudités, 2
Caramel
  -Coffee Sauce, 92
  -Cognac Fondue, 90-91
Cauliflower
  and Broccoli with Lemon, Mustard and Chive
    Butter, 76
  Potatoes and Peas, Indian, 82-83
Caviar, Red, Dip, 6
Cheese
  Blue Cheese Dip with Pecans, 3
  Camembert with Blue Cheese, Figs and
    Port Sauce, 4
  Caraway, Black Pepper and Parmesan Butter,
    Peas with, 74
  Chicken and Mushroom Quesadillas, 13
  Crostini with Gorgonzola and Figs, 6-7
  and Double-Corn Muffins, 87
  Duck Sausage Pizza with Green Onions and
    Tomato, 67-68
  Endive and Pear Salad with Gorgonzola Cream
    Dressing, 26
  Fettuccine Quatro Formaggi, 58
  Flatbread Pizzas with Olives, Feta and
    Artichokes, 66
  Garlic Bread with Pecorino Romano Butter, 85
  Goat Cheese and Watercress Tea Sandwiches, 64

  Grilled Blue Cheese Sandwiches with Walnuts
    and Watercress, 63
  Grilled Bread Topped with Arugula, Goat Cheese,
    Olives and Onions, 3
  Gruyère Fondue with Salsa Verde, 51-52
  Mexican-Style Chicken Sandwiches, 68
  Parmesan Toasts, 22-23
  Pasta with Greens, Goat Cheese and Raisins, 54
  Polenta with Fresh Herbs and White Cheddar
    Cheese, 84
  Tomatoes and Feta Cheese with Herb-and-Garlic
    Dressing, 25
  Turkey Tenderloins with Pesto and Provolone
    Cheese, 44-45
Cherries Jubilee, Triple, 91-92
Chicken
  Breasts, Cornmeal-Crusted, 42
  Cacciatore, Spicy, 41
  and Green Onions, Spicy Grilled, 44
  with Herbed Vegetable Sauce, 41-42
  and Mushroom Quesadillas, 13
  with Mustard Cream on Watercress, 44
  Orange and Ginger, 43
  and Pasta Salad, Southwestern, 33
  Salad Bar Cobb, 33
Chocolate
  Candy Cane Hot White Chocolate, 18
  Chip and Peanut Butter Cookies, Flourless, 93
  Hot Cocoa with Coffee Liqueur, 14
  Mocha-Chip Cookies, 93

Coffee
-Caramel Sauce, 92
Mocha-Chip Cookies, 93
Cookies
Flourless Peanut Butter and Chocolate Chip, 93
Mocha-Chip, 93
Corn
Bread, Old-Fashioned, 84
Double-Corn and Cheese Muffins, 87
and Winter Squash with Spinach and Bacon, 75
Cornmeal
Chili Muffins, 85
-Crusted Chicken Breasts, 42
Old-Fashioned Corn Bread, 84

Desserts
Caramel-Cognac Fondue, 90-91
Coffee-Caramel Sauce, 92
Flourless Peanut Butter and Chocolate Chip
Cookies, 93
Fresh Fruit Salad with Honey, Mint and Lime
Syrup, 90
Mocha-Chip Cookies, 93
Red, White and Blue Ice Cream Sundaes, 92
Strawberry and Macaroon Parfaits, 90
Tiramisù Angel Cake Torte, 94
Triple-Cherries Jubilee, 91-92
Dip(s)
Asian-Style, for Crudités, 4

Beef and Broccoli Wontons with Ginger
Dipping Sauce, 11
Blue Cheese, with Pecans, 3
Caesar, with Crudités, 2
Honey-Mustard, for Asparagus and Sugar
Snap Peas, 2
Red Caviar, 6

Egg(s)
Deviled, with Curry, 8
Double-Salmon and Sweet Potato Hash with
Poached Eggs, 70-71
Huevos Rancheros, 70
Salad with Belgian Endive, 8
Shiitake Scrambled Eggs and Caviar on Toasts, 69
Endive
Apple and Parmesan Salad with Walnut
Vinaigrette, 27
Belgian Endive with Egg Salad, 8
and Pear Salad with Gorgonzola Cream
Dressing, 26

Fennel, Broiled, and Red Bell Pepper Salad, 25
Fig(s)
Camembert with Blue Cheese, Figs and Port
Sauce, 4
and Gorgonzola, Crostini with, 6-7
and Pork Cutlets with Balsamic Vinegar, 50-51

Fish. See also Shellfish
Brazilian Seafood Stew, 40-41
Cajun-Style Blackened Halibut, 37
Double-Salmon and Sweet Potato Hash with
Poached Eggs, 70-71
Sea Bass Crusted with Pepitas and Coriander, 38
Sea Bass with Shallots, Garlic and Marsala, 37
Smoked-Salmon Pizza with Red Onion and
Dill, 10
Smoked Salmon Tartare with Ginger and
Sesame, 9
Smoked Trout, Watercress and Apple Salad with
Creamy Horseradish Dressing, 32
Tuna and Vegetable Fettuccine with Lemon
Breadcrumbs, 55
Tuna Pepper Steaks, Seared, 36
Fondue
Caramel-Cognac, 90-91
Gruyère, with Salsa Verde, 51-52
Fruit(s). See also kinds of fruits
Fresh Fruit Salad with Honey, Mint and Lime
Syrup, 90

Green Bean(s)
with Mushroom-Madeira Sauce, 78
and Red Bell Peppers with Marjoram and
Almonds, 76
Spinach and Pear Salad with Riesling Dressing, 24

Hearts of Palm Salad with Olives and Ham, 27-28
Huevos Rancheros, 70
Hummus, Butter Bean and Cumin, 5-6

Ice Cream
   Red, White and Blue Ice Cream Sundaes, 92
   Triple-Cherries Jubilee, 91-92

Kiwi and Asian Pear Salsa, Lamb Chops with, 50

Lamb
   Chops with Asian Pear and Kiwi Salsa, 50
   Rack of Lamb, with Spice-and-Pepper Crust, 51
Leeks
   Green Beans with Mushroom-Madeira Sauce, 78
   and Scallops in Star Anise-Orange Sauce, 10
Lima Bean, Artichoke and Pea Salad, 28

Macaroni Salad, Modern, 31
Mango-Boysenberry Mimosa, 15
Marmalade, Orange, Five-Minute Spiced, 88
Meat(s). See Bacon; Beef; Chicken; Lamb;
   Pork; Sausage; Turkey; Veal
Muffins, Double-Corn and Cheese, 87
Mushroom(s)
   and Chicken Quesadillas, 13
   -Madeira Sauce, Green Beans with, 78

Penne with Sausage, Wild Mushrooms and
   Spinach, 58
Penne with Turkey and Wild Mushrooms, 59-60
Roasted Vegetables with Garlic-Tarragon
   Butter, 78-79
Shiitake Scrambled Eggs and Caviar on Toasts, 69
Squash and Bell Pepper Salad, 23
   and Tomatoes, Veal Cutlets with, 48

Nuts. See Pecans; Walnuts

Onion(s)
   Green Onion Biscuits, 86-87
   Grilled Bread Topped with Arugula, Goat Cheese,
      Olives and Onions, 3
   Smoked-Salmon Pizza with Red Onion and
      Dill, 10
Orange(s)
   and Ginger Chicken, 43
   Mango-Boysenberry Mimosa, 15
   Marmalade, Spiced, Five-Minute, 88

Pancakes
   Buttermilk, with Blueberry Compote, 71-72
   Zucchini-Currant, 72
Pasta
   and Chicken Salad, Southwestern, 33
   Fettuccine Quatro Formaggi, 58

Fusilli with Fresh Tomato and Olive Sauce, 54-55
   with Greens, Goat Cheese and Raisins, 54
Linguine with Sun-Dried Tomato Pesto, 56
Macaroni Salad, Modern, 31
Orzo Pilaf with Green Onions and Parmesan
   Cheese, 83
Peanut Noodles with Gingered Vegetables
   and Tofu, 57
Penne with Sausage, Wild Mushrooms and
   Spinach, 58
Penne with Shrimp, Asparagus and Sun-Dried
   Tomatoes, 60
Penne with Turkey and Wild Mushrooms, 59-60
Spicy Asian-Style Pasta Salad, 30
Spicy Sesame and Ginger Noodle Salad, 29
Szechuan Sesame Noodles, 83
   with Tomatoes, Zucchini and Pesto, 53
Tuna and Vegetable Fettuccine with Lemon
   Breadcrumbs, 55
Pea(s)
   Artichoke and Lima Bean Salad, 28
   with Caraway, Black Pepper and Parmesan
      Butter, 74
   and Green Onions, Risotto with, 59
   Potatoes and Cauliflower, Indian, 82-83
   Sautéed Radishes and Sugar Snap Peas, 75
   Sugar Snap Peas and Asparagus with Honey-
      Mustard Dip, 2
Peanut Butter
   and Chocolate Chip Cookies, Flourless, 93

Peanut Dressing, Spicy-Sweet, 30-31
Peanut Sauce, Chinese, 57
Pear(s)
    and Endive Salad, with Gorgonzola Cream
        Dressing, 26
    Lamb Chops with Asian Pear and Kiwi Salsa, 50
    Spinach and Green Bean Salad with Riesling
        Dressing, 24
Pecans
    Blue Cheese Dip with, 3
    Garlic and Basil, Brussels Sprouts with, 77
    Sweet and Spicy, 13
Pepitas
    and Coriander, Sea Bass Crusted with, 38
    Sugar and Spice, 9-10
Pesto, Sun-Dried Tomato, Linguine with, 56
Pizza(s)
    Duck Sausage, with Green Onions and
        Tomato, 67-68
    Flatbread Pizzas with Olives, Feta and
        Artichokes, 66
    Smoked Salmon, with Red Onion and Dill, 10
Polenta with Fresh Herbs and White Cheddar
    Cheese, 84
Pork Cutlets with Figs and Balsamic Vinegar, 50-51
Potato(es)
    Dill Mashed, with Crème Fraîche and
        Caviar, 81
    Mashed, with Lemon and Chives, 80
    Mashed, with Prosciutto and Parmesan
        Cheese, 79-80
    Peas and Cauliflower, Indian, 82-83
    Salad, French, 27

Poultry. See Chicken; Turkey

Quesadillas, Chicken and Mushroom, 13

Radishes and Sugar Snap Peas, Sautéed, 75
Ranch Dressing, 21
Rice. See Risotto
Risotto
    with Peas and Green Onions, 59
    with Spicy Sausage, 12

Salad(s), 21-35
    Apple, Endive and Parmesan Salad with Walnut
        Vinaigrette, 27
    Artichoke, Lima Bean and Pea, 28
    Asian-Style Pasta Salad, Spicy, 30
    Broiled Fennel and Red Bell Pepper, 25
    Chicken and Pasta, Southwestern, 33
    Cobb, Salad Bar, 33
    Confetti, with Ranch Dressing, 21
    Country Beet, 28-29
    Crab, with Sun-Dried Tomato Louis Dressing, 34
    Endive and Pear, with Gorgonzola Cream
        Dressing, 26
    Hearts of Palm, with Olives and Ham, 27-28
    Macaroni, Modern, 31
    Mushroom, Squash and Bell Pepper, 23
    Potato, French, 27
    Sesame and Ginger Noodle, Spicy, 29

Smoked Trout, Watercress and Apple, with
    Creamy Horseradish Dressing, 32
Spinach, Pear and Green Bean, with Riesling
    Dressing, 24
Tomatoes and Feta Cheese with Herb-and-Garlic
    Dressing, 25
Waldorf, 29-30
Warm Spinach, with Parmesan Toasts, 22-23
Winter Greens with Grapefruit Vinaigrette, 23
Salad Dressing(s)
    Creamy Horseradish, for Smoked Trout,
        Watercress and Apple Salad, 32
    Gorgonzola Cream Dressing, for Endive and
        Pear Salad, 26
    Grapefruit Vinaigrette, Winter Greens with, 23
    Herb-and-Garlic, for Tomatoes and Feta
        Cheese, 25
    Ranch, 22
    Riesling, for Spinach, Pear and Green Bean
        Salad, 24
    Spicy-Sweet Peanut Dressing, 30-31
    Tomato Louis, for Crab Salad, 34
    Walnut Vinaigrette, for Apple, Endive and
        Parmesan Salad, 27
    Zinfandel, 32
Salsa(s)
    Asian Pear and Kiwi, Lamb Chops with, 50
    Salsa Verde, Gruyère Fondue with, 51-52
Sandwiches
    The Best BLTs, 61
    Black Bean and Vegetable Wraps, 65-66
    Chicken, Mexican-Style, 68

Goat Cheese and Watercress Tea Sandwiches, 64
Grilled Blue Cheese, with Walnuts and
    Watercress, 63
Hamburgers with Mustard and Mixed Herbs, 62
Peanut Butter, Banana and Date, 64
Smoked-Turkey Tea Sandwiches with Arugula
    Mayonnaise, 63
Spicy Turkey Sloppy Joes, 65
Sausage
    and Beef Tacos, Spicy, 66-67
    Duck Sausage Pizza with Green Onions and
        Tomato, 67-68
    Spicy, Risotto with, 12
    Wild Mushrooms and Spinach, Penne with, 58
Seafood. *See* Fish; Shellfish
Shellfish
    Brazilian Seafood Stew, 40-41
    Crab Salad with Sun-Dried Tomato Louis
        Dressing, 34
    Mussels with Pernod and Cream, 40
    Shrimp, Asparagus and Sun-Dried Tomatoes,
        Penne with, 60
    Shrimp, Sautéed with Lemon-Garlic
        Butter, 38-39
Soup(s)
    Black Bean, Quick, 20-21
    Creamy Zucchini, 20
    Zucchini and Dill, 21
Spinach
    and Bacon, with Corn and Winter Squash, 75
    Pear and Green Bean Salad with Riesling
        Dressing, 24

Salad, Warm, with Parmesan Toasts, 22
Sausage and Wild Mushrooms, Penne with, 58
Squash. *See also* Zucchini
    Corn and Winter Squash with Spinach and
        Bacon, 75
Strawberry and Macaroon Parfaits, 90
Sweet Potato and Double-Salmon Hash with
    Poached Eggs, 70-71

Tacos, Spicy Beef and Sausage, 66-67
Tomato(es)
    The Best BLTs, 61
    and Feta Cheese with Herb-and-Garlic
        Dressing, 25
    and Mushrooms, Veal Cutlets with, 48
    and Olive Sauce, Fusilli with, 54-55
    Zucchini and Pesto, Pasta with, 53
Torte, Tiramisù Angel Cake, 94
Turkey
    Salad Bar Cobb, 33
    Sloppy Joes, Spicy, 65
    Smoked-Turkey Tea Sandwiches with Arugula
        Mayonnaise, 63
    Tenderloins with Pesto and Provolone
        Cheese, 44-45
    and Wild Mushrooms, Penne with, 59-60

Veal
    Chops with Arugula Salad, 48-49
    Cutlets with Mushrooms and Tomatoes, 48

Vegetable(s). *See also kinds of vegetables*
    and Black Bean Wraps, 65-66
    Caesar Dip with Crudités, 2
    Confetti Salad with Ranch Dressing, 21
    Crudités with Asian-Style Dip, 4
    Peanut Noodles with Gingered Vegetables
        and Tofu, 57
    Roasted, with Garlic-Tarragon Butter, 78-79

Walnut(s)
    Vinaigrette, for Apple, Endive and Parmesan
        Salad, 27
    and Watercress, Grilled Blue Cheese Sandwiches
        with, 63
Watercress
    and Goat Cheese Tea Sandwiches, 64
    Smoked Trout, Watercress and Apple Salad with
        Creamy Horseradish Dressing, 32
    and Walnuts, Grilled Blue Cheese Sandwiches
        with, 63

Yams Braised with Cream, Rosemary and
    Nutmeg, 81

Zucchini
    -Currant Pancakes, 72
    and Dill Soup, 21
    Mushroom, Squash and Bell Pepper Salad, 23
    Soup, Creamy, 20
    Tomatoes and Pesto, Pasta with, 53

Acknowledgements & Credits

Recipes supplied by:
Bruce Aidells
Amy Auburn
Brad Avooske
Mary Corpening Barber
Melanie Barnard
Bonnie Bennett
Georgeanne Brennan
Joan Brett
Lisa Calazzo
Lane Crowther
Michel Depardon
Brooke Dojny

Crescent Dragonwagon
Suzanne Dunaway
Kara & Jeremiah Evarts
Janet Fletcher
Monique Gaspais
Grace Gordon
Sophie Grigson
Kathy Gunst
Russell Ito
Mollie Katzen
Sarah & Paul Kelth
Jeanne Thiel Kelley
Norman Kolpas

Rebecca Levy
Donata Maggipinto
Michael McLaughlin
Erin Renouf Myirole
Rochelle Palermo
Christine Piccin
Anita Ravon
Mary Risley
Rick Rodgers
Betty Rosbottom
Margaret Jane Ross
Etta Lou Schenzinger
Tracy Scott

Deborah Serangell
Stacey Siegal
Jeanne Silvestri
Prem K. Singh
Susan Springob
Lori &Kurt Stuckman
Sarah Tenaglia
Mary Vaughan
Sara Corpening Whiteford
Mike Wilson
B.A. Test Kitchen

Text:
James Badham
Mark Bittman
Sarah Derbyshire
Dorie Greenspan
Sophie Grigson
Nicole Harb

Jim Henderson
Julie King
Norman Kolpas
Laura Samuel Meyn
Mark Miller
Katie O'Kennedy

Concept:
Linda Alexander
Susan Blattman
Todd Ilberg
Widiyana Sudirman

Editorial development and original writing:
Norman Kolpas

Graphic Design:
Sandy Douglas

Illustrations:
Michelle Burchard

Index:
Barbara Wurf

Proofreader:
Katie Goldman

Rights and permissions:
Sybil Shimazu Neubauer

Typography:
TeleText Typography, Inc.